A QUICK COURSE IN

MICROSOFT®

OFFICE

VERSION 4.3

For Windows®

Computer training books for busy people

JOYCE COX

POLLY URBAN

AN ONLINE PRESS BOOK

PUBLISHED BY
Online Press Incorporated
14320 NE 21st Street, Suite 18
Bellevue, WA 98007
(206) 641-3434, (800) 854-3344

Publisher's Cataloging in Publication
(Prepared by Quality Books Inc.)

Cox, Joyce.
    A quick course in Microsoft Office for Windows / Joyce Cox, Polly Urban.
    p. cm.
    Covers Word 6 for Windows, Excel 5, Access 2, PowerPoint 4.
    Includes index.
    Preassigned LCCN: 95-68957
    ISBN: 1-879399-39-3

    1. Microsoft Office for Windows.   2. Microsoft Word for Windows.
3. Microsoft Excel for Windows.   4. Microsoft Access.   5. Microsoft
PowerPoint for Windows.   6. Business--Computer programs.   7. Word
processing.   8. Electronic spreadsheets.   9. Computer graphics.
10. Database management.   11. Integrated software.   I. Urban, Polly.
II. Title.

    HF5548.5.M525C69 1995   005.369
                                       QBI95-20219
              Library of Congress Catalog Card Number 95-68957

Printed and bound in the United States of America

1 2 3 4 5 6 7 8 9 O F F I 3 2 1 0

Acknowledgment
For this book, we enlisted the help of our colleague Christina Dudley, who whipped the Word chapters into shape, wrestled with the layout, and tracked the project through to its final deadline. Many thanks, C.

Contents

1

Microsoft Office Basics

May 24, 1995

Ima Houseman, President
Tip Top Roofing, Inc.
4239 East Lake Avenue
Lakewood, WA 98403

RE: 1995 CARSON AWARDS

Dear Ms. Houseman:

I am pleased to be the bearer of good news! Yesterday, the Carson Committee voted unanimously to present one of its 1995 awards to your company, **Tip Top Roofing**. Your efforts during the past year to forge the industry alliances needed for a successful asphalt-shingle recycling program are an impressive demonstration of Tip Top Roofing's ongoing commitment to the environment.

As you know, the prestigious Carson Awards recognize companies who work to ensure that their business practices are environmentally sensitive. This year's awards will be presented at the Carson Gala Dinner on Friday July 28, 1995. I will contact you next week with further details.

Again, congratulations!

Ted Lee

As you probably know, Microsoft Office for Windows is a *suite* of applications that are also available as independent programs. The concept of suites is not new. In fact, Microsoft Office for the Mac was first introduced in 1988, with Office for Windows following in 1990. Two years later Lotus introduced its SmartSuite, and more recently Novell released PerfectOffice. We mention the competing suites because they have significantly influenced the development of Office. Originally Office consisted of separate applications that were simply bundled together as a marketing strategy. Although people were fairly eager to buy Office because of the perceived value for money, after the introduction of SmartSuite, Microsoft started responding to user requests that the Office products work better together. The result is a tightly integrated suite that as a whole is much more powerful than the sum of its component applications.

So let's take a closer look at the suite in question. Microsoft Office comes in two flavors: Standard and Professional. Both versions include the following primary applications:

Microsoft Word

- **Microsoft Word.** This award-winning word processor lets us write, edit, and print text documents. We can control the look of the text by changing the font, style, and size of its characters and by setting such elements as indents, line spacing, tabs, and margins. And we can check the accuracy of our words using the built-in spelling and grammar checkers.

Microsoft Excel

- **Microsoft Excel.** This spreadsheet lets us use efficient, built-in functions as shortcuts for performing mathematical, financial, and statistical calculations. These calculations can be as simple as totaling a row or column of values or as complex as figuring the rate of return on an investment under varying circumstances.

Microsoft PowerPoint

- **Microsoft PowerPoint.** This presentation program lets us put together sophisticated slide shows or electronic presentations with professional-looking graphic effects. We can format the slide text in a variety of eye-catching ways and add charts, tables, and pictures for even greater impact.

Microsoft Mail

- **Microsoft Mail.** Although the software for this popular e-mail package is not included with Office, the product does come with a license to use Mail on the workstation where Office is installed. If your workgroup is using Microsoft Mail, this license allows you to copy the necessary software to your machine.

Microsoft Office Professional adds one more application to this set (Office Standard users can ignore references to this program):

- **Microsoft Access.** This database lets us store and organize information in sets of tables. After creating a database, we can look at the information as a list (in columns and rows), or we can look at each item of information in a form, as though it were recorded on an index card. We can perform calculations and compute statistics such as totals and averages. And we can sort the information, find specific items, and create reports.

Microsoft Access

In addition to these primary applications, both Office Standard and Office Professional come with the following set of smaller applications that we can use to enhance our documents:

Supporting programs

- **Microsoft Graph,** which we use to turn tabular data into graphs and charts.

- **ClipArt Gallery,** a collection of ready-made graphics that we can import into any of the primary applications.

- **Microsoft Organization Chart,** which provides the tools for creating diagrams such as organization charts.

- **WordArt,** which enables us to mold text into various shapes for logos, banners, and headlines.

- **Equation Editor,** which enables us to correctly format complex equations.

This book is a fast-paced introduction to Microsoft Office. We start with a general introduction that covers some of the basic skills used in all the applications. Then we devote two chapters to each of the four primary tools. Finally, one chapter shows how to recycle information from one application to another for maximum efficiency. In 272 pages, we can't hope to cover all the ins and outs of Office and we don't try to. But we don't just skim the surface, sticking with the easy stuff. We focus on the most useful features—the ones most people will use most often

About this book

and the ones more people would use if they knew how. By the time you finish this Quick Course®, you'll have a firm understanding of the important features of Word, Excel, PowerPoint, and Access, and you'll know enough about Office to start experimenting on your own with the features we don't cover in detail. What's more you'll have created real documents that will serve as models for those you'll need to generate on the job, at school, or for personal use.

Getting Started

Because of all its components, you might think that Office would be difficult to master. Not so. An important aspect of this integrated suite is that you use the same commands and techniques in all the applications to carry out common tasks. Though each application has a particular focus, the techniques for tasks such as editing, formatting, saving, and printing are similar, and the experience you acquire with one application can be applied to another. For the rest of this chapter, we work with Word to create a letter. In the process, you learn basic techniques for working with all the Office applications.

Common commands and techniques

We assume that you've installed Office on your computer and that you allowed the Office Setup program to stash everything in the MSOFFICE directory on your hard disk, create a Microsoft Office group, and put the Microsoft Office icon in the Startup group so that Office is automatically started every time you load Windows. We also assume that you've worked with Windows before. If you are new to Windows, we recommend you take a look at *A Quick Course in Windows*, another book in the Quick Course series, which will help you quickly come up to speed.

Using MOM to Start an Application

Well, let's get going. With Windows loaded, the screen looks something like this:

Automatic Office

If Microsoft Office is not automatically loaded when you start Windows, you can start it by double-clicking the Microsoft Office icon in Program Manager's Microsoft Office group window. To have Office start automatically, open the StartUp group window, move it so that you can see the Microsoft Office icon, hold down the Ctrl key, and drag a copy of the icon into the StartUp group window. Shut down Windows and then restart it. When Windows is loaded, it will start Microsoft Office.

Microsoft Office Manager (MOM)

Notice the six buttons in the Program Manager title bar. (If you're working with Office Standard, you do not have an Access button—the one with the key.) These buttons comprise the Office control center, which is called the *Microsoft Office Manager*, or <u>MOM</u>. As you'll see, no matter which application we are working with, MOM is always visible at the top of the screen, allowing us to easily start one of the Office applications or to switch to that application if it is already loaded. Let's experiment:

Microsoft Office Manager (MOM)

1. Point to each MOM button in turn, pausing until the button's name appears in a box below the pointer. You can use this helpful feature, which is called *ToolTips*, to identify buttons in all the Office applications.

ToolTips

2. Click the Microsoft Word button to start Word.

The Microsoft Word button

3. If you see a window containing the "Tip of the Day," read the tip, click the Show Tips At Startup check box to deselect it, and click OK. (You can display tips at any time by choosing Tip Of The Day from the Help menu.) Your screen now looks like the one shown on the next page.

Control menu icon   *Menu bar*   *Title bar*

Standard toolbar

Formatting toolbar

Ruler

Insertion point

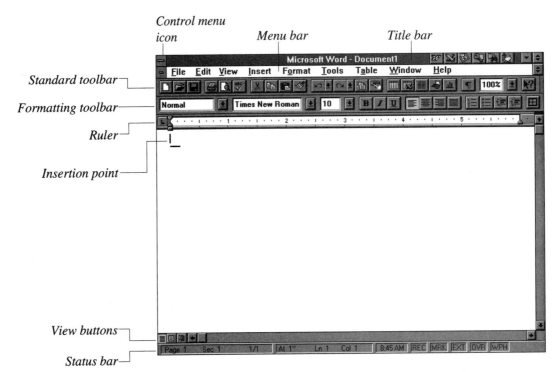

View buttons

Status bar

You'll learn what all the labeled parts of the window are as we work our way through this chapter. For now, just notice that MOM is still visible in the same location at the top of the screen.

Entering Text

Let's start by writing a paragraph. Follow these steps:

Insertion point

1. The blinking *insertion point* indicates where the next character you type will appear on the screen. Type the following:

   I am pleased to be the bearer of good news! Yesterday, the Carson Committee voted unanimously to present one of its 1995 awards to your company, Tip Top Roofing. Your efforts during the past year to forge the industry alliances needed for a successful asphalt-shingle recycling program are an impressive demonstration of Tip Top Roofing's ongoing commitment to the environment.

As each line of text reaches the right edge of the screen, the next word you type moves to a new line. This is called *word wrapping*. When entering text in Word and PowerPoint, you don't have to worry about pressing the Enter key to end one line and start another. The applications take care of that chore for you,

Correcting mistakes

We show you some simple editing techniques on page 19 but in the meantime, if you make a mistake and want to correct it, simply press the Backspace key until you've deleted the error and retype the text.

filling each line with as many words as will fit. (As you follow our examples, don't worry if your word wrapping isn't identical to ours.)

2. Press Enter to end the paragraph. Your screen looks like this:

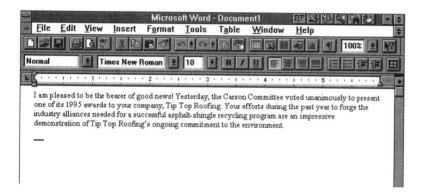

Now that we have some text on the screen, let's see what we can do with it.

Selecting Text

Before we can do much with this paragraph, we need to discuss how to select text. In all the Office applications, knowing how to select text efficiently saves time because we can then edit or format all the selected text at once, instead of a letter or word at a time. The simplest way to learn how to select text is to actually do it, so follow these steps to select some text blocks:

1. Move the pointer to the word *unanimously* and double-click it. The word changes to white on black (called *highlighting*) to indicate that it is selected:

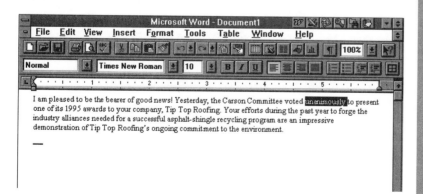

Whole word selection

By default, Word selects whole words. For example, if you start a selection in the middle of a word and drag beyond the last character, Word selects the entire word. If you drag to the first character of the next word, Word selects that word, and so on. You can tell Word to select only the characters you drag across by choosing Options from the Tools menu, clicking the Edit tab, clicking the Automatic Word Selection option to deselect it, and clicking OK.

Selecting by Shift-clicking

2. Point to the left of *Tip* and click the left mouse button to position the insertion point at the beginning of the word. Then point to the right of *Roofing*, hold down the Shift key, and click the left mouse button. (This action is sometimes referred to as *Shift-clicking*.) Word highlights the words between the two clicks:

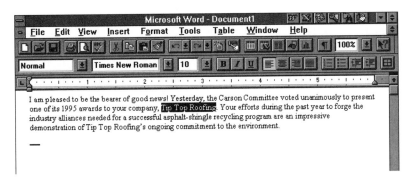

Selecting by dragging

3. Point to the left of the word *recycling*, hold down the left mouse button, drag to the right until *recycling program* is selected, and release the mouse button. Using this technique, you can highlight exactly as much or as little text as you need.

Extending a selection with the Shift key

4. Click an insertion point before the *Y* in *Yesterday*. Hold down the Shift key, press the Right Arrow key until the entire word is highlighted, and release the Shift key.

5. Without moving the selection, hold down the Shift key, press the Down Arrow key, and then press the Right Arrow key until the entire sentence is highlighted, like this:

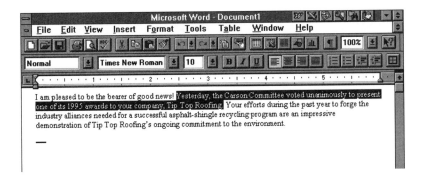

6. Next, try pressing different Arrow keys while holding down the Shift key. As long as you press Shift, Word extends the selection in the direction of the key's arrow.

7. Release the Shift key and press Home to move the insertion point to the beginning of the line where the selection starts and also remove any highlighting.

With slight variations, the techniques we've covered so far can be used in all the Office applications. The next selection technique, however, applies only to Word and PowerPoint:

1. Move the mouse pointer to the far left side of the window. When the pointer changes to an arrow, it is in an invisible vertical strip called the *selection bar*.

Selecting in the selection bar

2. Position the arrow pointer in the selection bar adjacent to the line that contains the words *Tip Top Roofing* and click the left mouse button once. Word highlights the line:

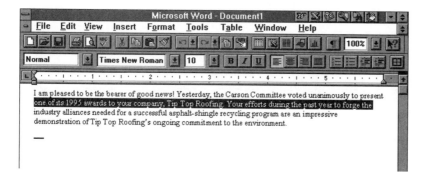

3. Now highlight the entire paragraph by double-clicking in the selection bar next to the paragraph.

We can also drag the pointer in the selection bar to select multiple lines or paragraphs.

Giving Instructions

Now that you know how to select text, let's discuss how we tell the Office applications what to do with the selection. We give instructions by clicking buttons and boxes on toolbars, by choosing menu commands, and by pressing keyboard shortcuts.

Using the Toolbars

Each Office application comes with a set of toolbars. At the moment, we can see Word's Standard and Formatting toolbars, which sport buttons and boxes that perform tasks related to word processing, but we can display other toolbars at any time. We can also hide the toolbars if we need to view more of a document at once. Let's explore the toolbars:

1. Familiarize yourself with the buttons and boxes on the two toolbars by moving the pointer slowly over each one so that ToolTips displays its name. (A brief description of each button's function also appears in the status bar at the bottom of your screen.)

2. Use any of the methods discussed on page 7 to select the first occurrence of *Tip Top Roofing*.

The Bold and Underline buttons

3. Click the Bold button on the Formatting toolbar and then click the Underline button. (You could also add italic formatting by clicking the Italic button.)

4. Press Home to remove the highlighting. As you can see, these two simple changes have a dramatic effect:

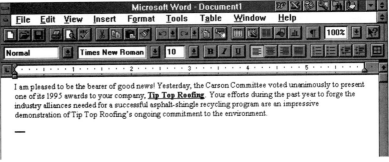

Now let's experiment with the document's font and font size:

Times New Roman

The Font box

1. Select the paragraph and click the arrow to the right of the Font box to display a list of the available fonts.

2. Use the scroll bar to the right of the drop-down box to bring the top of the list into view and then click Arial. The font of the text changes, and the setting in the Font box now reflects the new font.

10

The Font Size box

3. With the paragraph still selected, click the arrow to the right of the Font Size box, and then click 12 in the drop-down list.

4. Now press End so that you can see the results:

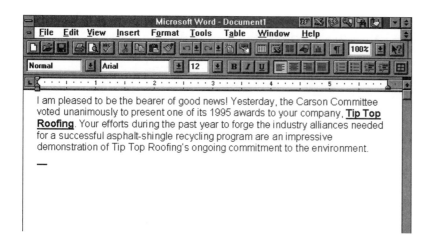

We have just used toolbar buttons and boxes to apply common character formats to a text selection. *Character formats* affect the appearance of individual characters. They can be applied to any number of characters, from one to the whole document. In Word, Excel, and PowerPoint, we can also use toolbar buttons to change *paragraph formats* which, as their name suggests, affect the appearance of an entire paragraph. Let's see how changing the alignment of a paragraph affects the way it looks:

Character formats

Paragraph formats

1. Press Ctrl+Home to move to the beginning of the document and then type the following, pressing Enter to end paragraphs and create blank lines where indicated, and pressing Enter twice after the salutation:

Moving to the beginning of a document

May 24, 1995 (Press Enter)
(Press Enter)
Ima Houseman, President (Press Enter)
Tip Top Roofing, Inc. (Press Enter)
4239 East Lake Avenue (Press Enter)
Lakewood, WA 98403 (Press Enter)
(Press Enter)
RE: 1995 CARSON AWARDS (Press Enter)
(Press Enter)
Dear Ms. Houseman: (Press Enter twice)

2. Press Crtl+Home and click the Align Right button to right-align the date.

The Align Right button

The Center button

3. Click an insertion point anywhere in the subject (*RE:*) line and then click the Center button. Here are the results:

Using Menu Commands

Most of the buttons on the toolbars have equivalent commands on the Office application menus, which are arranged on a menu bar that spans the screen below the title bar of each Office application. The menus on the menu bar are designed so that once we are familiar with the menu location of the commands in one Office application, we know where to find the same commands in any other Office application. Just as the applications' toolbars have some buttons that are the same and some that vary with each application, the applications' menus have some commands that are the same and some that vary.

Buttons vs. commands

So when do we use a button and when do we use a command? We can always use a command to carry out a particular task, but we can't always use a corresponding button. Clicking the button carries out its associated command with its predefined, or *default*, settings. When a command is not represented by a toolbar button, or when we want to use a command with something other than its default settings, we need to choose the command from a menu.

Help with commands

If you can't remember the name of the command you want to use, you can pull down each menu and press the Up Arrow and Down Arrow keys to highlight each command in turn. A brief description of the highlighted command appears in the window's status bar at the bottom of the screen.

Choosing Menu Bar Commands

Because the procedure for choosing menu commands is the same for all Windows applications, we assume that you are familiar with it. If you are a new Windows user, we suggest that you spend a little time becoming familiar with the mechanics of menus, commands, and dialog boxes before proceeding. Here, we'll run through the steps for choosing a command and do some useful exploring at the same time:

1. Click View on the menu bar to display this menu:

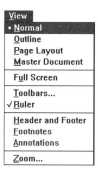

In all the Office applications, the View menu provides commands for customizing the screen display, but the actual commands vary from application to application. Notice that the Normal command has a dot in front of its name, indicating that, of the four commands above the first line on the menu, Normal is the command currently in effect. Choosing another of these four commands puts that command into effect and deactivates Normal. Notice also that the Ruler command has a check mark in front of its name, indicating that the command is a *toggle*. Choosing a checked toggle command turns off the command without affecting the status of any other command.

Mutually exclusive commands

Toggle commands

2. Choose the Ruler command from the View menu by clicking the name to turn off the ruler. (When you are working with a long document or with several documents at one time, you might want to turn off the ruler so that you can see more of your text. You can always open the menu and choose the command again to turn it back on.)

Turning off the Ruler

3. Click the View menu again (notice that Ruler no longer has a check mark) and choose Toolbars to display the dialog box shown on the next page.

Submenus

Excel, PowerPoint, and Access have several commands with right-pointing arrowheads next to their names on the menus. Choosing one of these commands displays a submenu of additional commands that you can choose simply by clicking them in the usual way. None of Word's commands have submenus.

Custom toolbars

You can customize toolbars by moving, removing, and adding buttons on any toolbar. Move a button by holding down the Alt key and dragging the button to its new position. (You can even drag from one toolbar to another.) Drag a copy of the button by holding down Alt+Ctrl. Remove a button by holding down Alt and dragging the button into the document window. To add a button, start by choosing Customize from the Tools menu. Select a category of actions from the Categories list to display the buttons available for that category, and then drag the button you want to the desired toolbar. To create a custom toolbar containing your favorite tools, or those you need for a specific task, choose Toolbars from the View menu, and click the New button. Assign a name in the Toolbar Name edit box, and specify which template you want to associate the toolbar with in the Make Toolbar Available To edit box. Click OK to display a new toolbar and the Customize dialog box, which you use as just described to add buttons to the custom toolbar. To delete a custom toolbar, choose Toolbars from the View menu, highlight the toolbar you want to delete, and click the Delete button (which is visible only when a custom toolbar is highlighted). You cannot undo this action. To return a toolbar to its default settings, choose Toolbars from the View menu, highlight the toolbar, and click Reset.

4. Click all the check boxes on the left side of the dialog box and click OK. Your screen now looks something like this:

(By pointing to their title bars, holding down the left mouse button, and dragging, we moved the two "floating" toolbars, Microsoft and Forms, so that they wouldn't obscure any of the other toolbars.)

5. Use ToolTips to get an idea of the names and functions of all the buttons on the new toolbars.

Choosing Shortcut Menu Commands

For efficiency, the commands that we are likely to use with a particular element of a file, such as a block of text, are combined on special menus, called *shortcut menus*. Shortcut menus are also available for window elements, such as the toolbars. We access an element's shortcut menu by pointing to that element and clicking the right mouse button. This action is called *right-clicking*. Try the following:

Right-clicking

1. Point to one of the toolbars, right-click to display the toolbar shortcut menu, and choose Borders from the menu to turn off the Borders toolbar.

2. Right-click a toolbar to display the shortcut menu again. You don't want to repeat step 1 to turn off the toolbars one at a time, so choose Toolbars from the bottom of the menu to display the dialog box you saw earlier, deselect all the check boxes except Standard and Formatting, and click OK.

Using Keyboard Shortcuts

We can't imagine anyone wanting to work with the Office applications using *only* the keyboard. Using a mouse makes working with most Windows applications much easier, and Office is no exception. However, if our hands are already on the keyboard, using keyboard shortcuts to access commands can be more efficient. We have already used the Ctrl+Home keyboard shortcut to move to the top of the document now on the screen. Here are a few more examples:

1. Select the subject line (RE: 1995 CARSON AWARDS) and press first Ctrl+B and then Ctrl+U to make the line bold and underlined. (You can achieve the same effect by clicking the Bold and Underline buttons on the Formatting toolbar.)

2. Now use a keyboard shortcut to change the alignment of the first paragraph you typed. Click an insertion point in the paragraph and press Ctrl+J to justify it so that its lines are even with both the left and right margins. (Pressing Ctrl+L left-aligns the paragraph, Ctrl+R right-aligns it, and Ctrl+E centers it.)

3. Press Ctrl+Home to move the insertion point to the top of the file. The results are shown on the next page.

Help with shortcuts

The list of keyboard shortcuts is extensive, and it would take a lot of space to reproduce it here. For more information about keyboard shortcuts, choose Index from the Help menu, and locate the Shortcuts entry. (See page 25 for more information about using the Help system.)

Saving Files

The Save button

Until we save a file on the hard disk, the file exists only in the computer's memory and disappears if the computer is intentionally or unintentionally turned off. Now would be a good time to save the document we have typed as a file. To save a new file, we click the Save button or choose Save As from the File menu to display a dialog box in which we specify the name of the file. Thereafter, clicking the Save button or choosing the Save command saves the file without displaying the dialog box because the file already has a name. Let's save the document now on the screen:

Filenames and extensions

Files are usually assigned a name and an extension separated by a period. Filenames cannot have more than eight characters, and extensions cannot have more than three. They can both consist of letters, numbers, and these characters:

_ ^ $ # % & - { } ( )

They can't contain spaces, commas, or periods.

1. Choose Save As from the File menu to display the Save As dialog box:

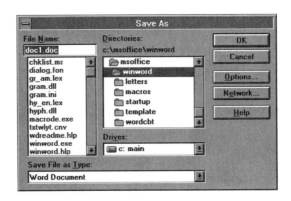

Word suggests *doc1.doc* as the name for the first document created in this Word session.

2. With *doc1.doc* highlighted, simply type *award1* in the File Name edit box. (If you don't supply an extension when saving a file, the Office applications automatically use extensions that associate the file with the program that created it. In this case, Word adds its DOC extension.)

3. Click OK. When you save a file for the first time, Word, Excel, and PowerPoint may display the Summary Info dialog box (if you don't see this dialog box, choose Summary Info from the File menu):

If you take the time to fill in summary information for your files, you can use the Find File command or Find File button (see page 233) to find the file later, when you may have forgotten what you named it and where you stored it. (If you don't anticipate using this method of finding files, you can choose Options from the Tools menu, click the Save tab, and deselect the Prompt For Summary Info option to tell the application not to display this dialog box.)

4. The Title edit box currently displays the first line of the document. Type *Tip Top Roofing* as the title, and in the Subject edit box, type *1995 Carson Awards*. Make sure your name appears in the Author edit box, type *award letter* in the Keywords edit box, and click OK to close the dialog box.

From now on, we can click the Save button any time we want to save changes to this file. Because the application knows the name of the file, it simply saves the file by overwriting the old version with the new version.

Saving in a different directory

The file will be saved in the directory designated by the path above the Directories list. For example, the path C:\MSOFFICE\WINWORD means that the file will be saved in the WINWORD subdirectory of the MSOFFICE directory on your C drive. If you want to store the file in a different directory, you need to switch to the correct directory before you click OK to save the file. Double-click a directory icon in the Directories list to select that directory, display its files in the File Name list, and display its subdirectories in the Directories list. Double-click a subdirectory icon to display its files and subdirectories, and so on.

Creating New Files

Part of the magic of a computer is that we can use the same information for different purposes without retyping the information each time. When we have already created one file and we want to adapt it for a different purpose without destroying the original, we can save the file with a new name to create a new file without destroying the old one. Try this:

Creating a new file based on an old one

1. Choose Save As from the File menu, replace the name in the File Name edit box by typing *award2*, and click OK. If necessary, click OK to close the Summary Info dialog box without entering any summary information. Word closes AWARD1.DOC, and the filename in the title bar changes to AWARD2.DOC.

We can create a totally new file at any time without closing any open files. Follow these steps:

The New button

1. Click the New button on the Standard toolbar. Word displays a new file called *Document2* on top of AWARD2.DOC.

2. Type the following paragraph, misspelling *Carson* as *Carsen* and pressing Enter only at the end:

   As you no doubt know, the prestigious Carsen Awards recognize companies who work to ensure that their business practices are sensitive environmentally. This year's awards will be presented at the Carsen Gala Dinner on Friday July 28, 1995. I will contact you next week with more details.

3. Save the file with the name *award3*.

Manipulating Windows

We now have a couple of open files in separate, stacked windows, so we'll pause here to review some window basics. Being able to work with more than one file open at a time is useful, especially if the files are related in some way. Follow these steps to see how easy it is to move from one document to another:

Activating an open file

1. Click Window on the menu bar to display the commands on the Window menu. The two open files are listed at the bottom of the menu, with a check mark beside AWARD3.DOC to indicate that its window is active.

2. Choose AWARD2.DOC from the list of open files. That file comes to the top of the stack of windows.

3. Choose Arrange All from the Window menu. The two open files arrange themselves so that they each occupy half of the screen, like this:

Arranging windows

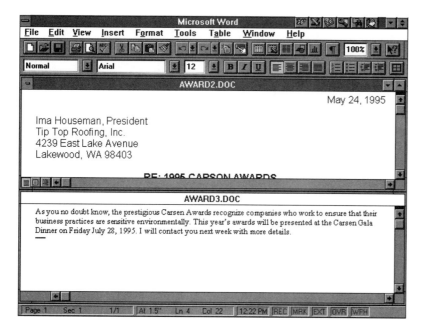

Notice that the title bar of the active file is darker than that of the inactive file. Any entries you make and most commands you choose will affect only the active file.

4. Click anywhere in AWARD3.DOC to activate it and then click the AWARD3.DOC window's Maximize button (the upward-pointing arrowhead at the right end of its title bar). The window expands to fill the screen, completely obscuring AWARD2.DOC.

Maximizing a window

Simple Editing

Typically when creating documents we will start by typing roughly what we want the document to contain and then we'll go back and edit the contents until we are satisfied with them.

In this section, we'll quickly cover the editing techniques that we can use in all the Office applications. (Because we are working in Word, we'll be dealing with text, but these techniques can be used with any type of entry.) Other techniques are covered in the chapters about specific applications.

Deleting and Replacing Text

First let's make a few small changes. Follow these steps:

1. Click an insertion point to the left of the *e* in the first occurrence of *Carsen*, press the Delete (Del) key to delete the character to the right, and without moving the insertion point, type *o*.

2. Click an insertion point to the right of the *e* in the second occurrence of *Carsen*, press the Backspace key to delete the character to the left, and again type *o*.

3. Select the words *no doubt* in the first line and press either Delete or Backspace to delete the words.

4. Double-click the word *more* in the last line and with the word highlighted, type *further* as its replacement.

5. Click the Save button to save AWARD3.DOC.

Moving and Copying Text

We can move or copy any amount of text within the same file or to a different file. Move operations can be carried out in all Office applications using the Cut and Paste buttons on the Standard toolbar. Similarly, copy operations can be carried out using the Copy and Paste buttons. Let's experiment:

The Cut button

1. In AWARD3.DOC, select the word *sensitive* and click the Cut button. Word removes the text from the document and stores it in a temporary storage place, called the *Clipboard*, in your computer's memory.

The Paste button

2. Click an insertion point to the right of the *y* in *environmentally* and click the Paste button. Word inserts the cut text, preceding it with a space.

Now let's try copying text to a different file:

1. Choose Select All from the Edit menu to select all the text in AWARD3.DOC and then click the Copy button.

The Copy button

2. Choose AWARD2.DOC from the Window menu to activate the letter.

3. Press Ctrl+End to move to the end of the letter, press Enter twice to add a blank line, and then click the Paste button to insert the selected paragraph.

As you can see, when we copied the paragraph from AWARD3 to AWARD2, we copied the formatting of the paragraph as well. We'll reformat the entire letter in a moment.

Undoing and Redoing Commands

For those occasions when we make an editing mistake, the Office applications provide a safety net: the Undo command. Try this:

1. You're not sure you need the paragraph you copied into the letter, so click the Undo button to reverse the paste operation from the previous steps.

The Undo button

2. Change your mind again, and click the Redo button to paste the paragraph back into the letter.

The Redo button

Printing Files

Whether we are writing a letter, generating a budget, producing a slide show, or extracting information from a database, the end product of many of our Office sessions will be a printout. If you can print from any other Windows application, you should have no trouble printing from the Office applications. First, let's finish off the letter:

1. With the insertion point at the end of the letter, press Enter to add a blank line, type *Again, congratulations!*, press Enter four times, type *Ted Lee*, and press Enter again.

Undoing and redoing multiple actions

In Word, you can undo and redo several actions at a time. Simply click the arrow to the right of the appropriate button and drag through the actions in the list that you want to undo or redo. You cannot undo or redo a single action other than the last one. For example, to undo the third action in the list, you must also undo the first and second.

The Justify button

2. Choose Select All from the Edit menu and change the Font setting on the Formatting toolbar to Times New Roman and the Font Size setting to 10.

3. Finally, select the second paragraph only and click the Justify button on the Formatting toolbar. The letter now looks like the one shown here:

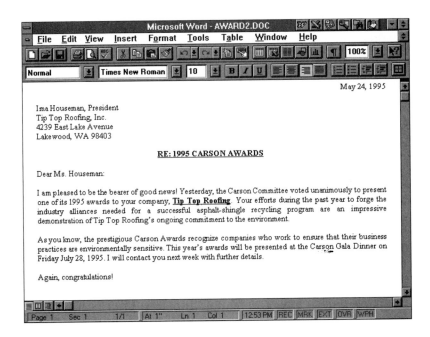

4. Save the letter.

Previewing Files

The letter we have written is only one page long and it has no headers or footers. However, it is worth checking even a file this small in print preview to get an idea of how it looks on the page. Follow these steps to preview the letter:

The Print Preview button

1. Click the Print Preview button on the Standard toolbar to display the entire page like this:

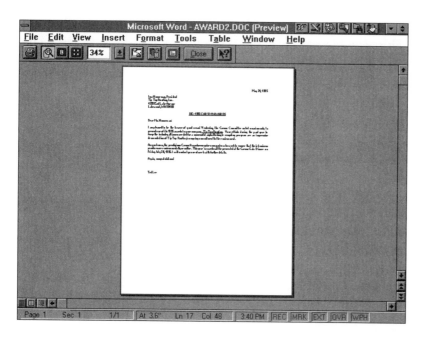

2. Move the mouse pointer over the letter and when the pointer changes to a magnifying glass, click the left mouse button to zoom in on the letter. Click the mouse button again to zoom out.

Zooming in and out

3. Click the Close button on the Print Preview toolbar to return to normal view.

Changing Page Layout

Let's modify the page layout so that the letter sits lower and takes up more of the page. These modifications are accomplished by widening the top and side margins, as you'll see if you follow these steps:

1. Choose Page Setup from the File menu to display this dialog box:

Adjusting margins

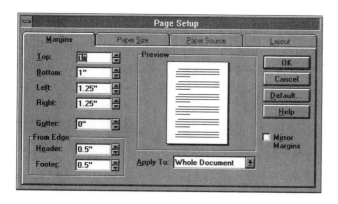

Tabbed dialog boxes

As you can see, Word's Page Setup dialog box is multilayered, with each layer designated at the top of the dialog box by a tab like a file folder tab. The Margins tab is currently displayed. (If it's not, click Margins at the top of the dialog box.)

2. With the Top Margin setting highlighted, type *1.5* and press Tab twice to skip over the Bottom Margin setting and highlight the Left Margin setting.

3. Type *1.5* as the new Left Margin setting, press Tab, type *1.5* as the new Right Margin setting, and press Tab again.

4. Notice the effects of your changes in the sample to the right and then click OK to return to the letter.

5. Click the Print Preview button to see how the letter looks.

6. Click Close to return to normal view.

Straightforward Printing

We can print directly from print preview by clicking the Print button on the Print Preview toolbar. Here's how to print a file from normal view:

The Print button

1. Click the Print button on the Standard toolbar. That's it! Word prints the active document with the default settings: one copy of all the pages in the document.

If we want to print multiple copies or print selected pages, we must use the Print command on the File menu instead of the Print button on the toolbar. Here's how:

1. Choose Print from the File menu to display this dialog box:

Setting up for printing

When you installed Windows, you indicated which printers you had available. These printers can all be accessed by your Office applications, but only one at a time. To switch printers, choose Print from the File menu and click the Printer or Printer Setup button. (In Access, choose Print Setup from the File menu instead.) Then select the printer you want and click OK.

Notice that the Print dialog box tells you which printer Office will use.

2. In the Copies edit box, type *2* to replace the default setting of 1. ← **Printing more than one copy**

3. Click the Pages option in the Page Range section and type *1-3* in the edit box to tell Word to print pages 1 through 3 only. ← **Printing a range of copies**

4. We aren't actually going to print using these specifications, so click Cancel to close the Print dialog box.

Rather than explain the other printing options in detail here, we'll move on to the next section, where we show you how to get information about these options and other features of the Office applications.

Getting Help

Are you worried that you might not remember everything we've covered so far? Don't be. If you forget how to carry out a particular task, help is never far away. You've already seen how the ToolTips feature and the descriptions in the status bar can jog your memory about the functions of the toolbar buttons. And you may have noticed that the Word, Excel, and PowerPoint dialog boxes contain a Help button you can click to get information about their options. Here we'll look at ways to get information using the application Help systems.

We can access the Help systems in several ways. First let's use the Help menu:

1. Choose Contents from the Help menu and, if necessary, click the Maximize button in the top-right corner of the window. Clicking any of the options in the Contents window takes you to topic lists that enable you to find the information you need.

2. Press the F1 key to get information about using Help and then click Move Around In Help in the list of How To topics. If you make a mistake, simply click the Back button to retrace your steps. Your screen looks like the one shown on the next page. ← **Getting help with Help**

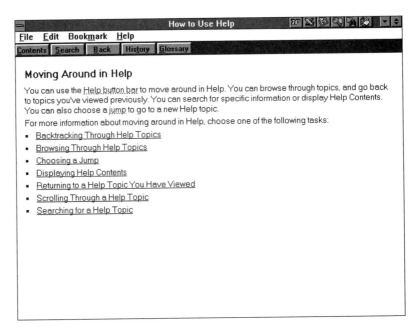

3. Click topics with dotted underscores to display pop-up definitions and topics with solid underscores to jump to related information. When you are finished, click the Back button until you return to the Contents window.

4. Explore any other Help topics that interest you.

Quitting Help

5. When you are ready, choose the Exit command from Help's File menu to return to your document.

To search for specific information in Help, follow these steps:

Searching for a topic

1. Choose Search For Help On from the Help menu to display this dialog box:

This dialog box can also be accessed by clicking the Search button on the Help window's toolbar.

2. In turn, press the P, R, and I keys. The Search list scrolls to display topics beginning with *pri*.

3. Select one of the print topics and then click the Show Topics button. A list of all the topics related to the selected subject is displayed in the bottom box of the Search window.

4. Select a topic and click the Go To button to jump directly to that Help topic.

5. Choose Exit from the File menu to leave Help.

We'll leave you to explore the other Help topics on your own.

Quitting

Well, that's it for the basic Office tour. We'll finish up by showing you how to quit first an application and then Office:

1. Choose Exit from the File menu. (Alternatively, you can double-click the Control menu icon at the left end of the application window's title bar, but that takes a little practice.)

Quitting applications

2. If the application asks whether you want to save the changes you have made to an open file, click Yes to save the changes or No to discard them. Click Yes in this case.

3. After the application closes, click the Microsoft Office button on the MOM toolbar and choose Exit from the menu that appears. You can then safely quit Windows and turn off your machine.

The Microsoft Office button

If you want to continue working without quitting Windows, you can click the Microsoft Office icon in Program Manager's Microsoft Office group window to restart Office and redisplay MOM.

The Microsoft Office icon

Word Basics

Assign heading levels and
reorganize your documents
in outline view

Redmond Business Environmental Action Team

What is Redmond BEAT?

Redmond BEAT (Business Environmental Action Team) is a local chapter of USA BEAT, a network of companies who are actively working to ensure that their business operations are based on sound environmental practices.

How does it work?

Member companies agree to participate in two ongoing efforts: 1. They pledge to scrutinize their operations and wherever possible, implement procedures that will minimize any adverse effects on the environment. 2. They agree to field-test new "environmentally kind" products and services to evaluate their potential impact on both company costs and the environment.

When was it started?

Redmond BEAT was founded in 1989. USA BEAT, which currently has 210 local chapters, was founded in 1987.

Why was it started?

The chartering of Redmond BEAT was spearheaded by long-time Redmond resident William Henry, President of Creative GlassWorks. Struck by the incongruity between his family's efforts to recycle household waste and the fact that his company was sending several dumpsters of garbage to the Redmond landfill every month, Henry began looking for other ways to dispose of the packaging in which his company received raw materials. His questions caused one of his suppliers, Jordan Manufacturing, to explore alternative packaging methods. The result was less garbage in the Creative GlassWorks dumpsters at no additional; cost and negligible other effects for either company. In the meantime, Henry learned about USA BEAT, and a few months of persuasive campaigning later, Redmond BEAT became the newest chapter of a rapidly growing national association.

Who can join?

Membership in Redmond BEAT is open to all companies licensed to do business in the city of Redmond.

Why should my company join?

Current members cite two main reasons for joining. Many companies are managed by people who were attracted to this area by its natural beauty and who want to be part of the effort to preserve it. Other companies stress the potential advantages in today's competitive markets of being perceived as a "green" company by consumers who are increasingly environmentally aware.

How can I find out more?

Come to a meeting. Redmond BEAT meets at 8:00 AM on the last Tuesday of every month in the Community Center. For more information, contact Ted Lee at 555-6789.

Find and replace
text to maintain
consistency

Use AutoText and
AutoCorrect for
often-used text

Check spelling to
avoid embarrassing
typos

Delete, move, and
copy text until it
reads exactly right

I n this chapter, we build on what you learned about Microsoft Office and Microsoft Word in Chapter 1. If you haven't read Chapter 1 and are new to Microsoft Word, you should read that chapter before proceeding with this one.

With Word, we can apply fancy formats and add graphics and special effects to increase the impact of a document. But all the frills in the world won't compensate for bad phrasing, bad organization, or errors. That's why this chapter focuses on the Word tools that help us develop and refine the content of our documents. As the example for this chapter, we create a "backgrounder" for an association called Redmond Business Environmental Action Team (BEAT). Backgrounders provide general information about a company or organization, and they are often mailed out with press releases and other promotional materials.

Backgrounders

First let's enter a few headings to establish the basic structure of the document:

1. If necessary, start Word by clicking MOM's Microsoft Word button. If Word is already loaded, a new document should be on the screen. If you have an existing document open, choose Close from the File menu and then click the New button on the toolbar to open a new blank document.

2. If necessary, turn off the ruler by choosing Ruler from the View menu. That way, you'll have a bit more room to work.

The Show/Hide ¶ button

3. Click the Show/Hide ¶ button on the toolbar, which displays nonprinting characters, such as paragraph marks and spaces.

4. Type *What is Redmond BEAT?* and press Enter. Word enters the heading, inserts a paragraph mark, and moves the insertion point to the next line.

5. Type *Why was it started?* and press Enter.

6. Continue entering the headings shown here (we've magnified the document to make it easier to read):

7. Now save the document by clicking the Save button, specifying *bkground* as the name of the file, and clicking OK.

Let's add some text under a couple of the headings:

1. Click an insertion point between the question mark and the paragraph mark at the end of the *What is Redmond BEAT?* heading, press Enter, and type the following:

   Redmond BEAT (Business Environmental Action Team) is a local chapter of National BEAT, a network of companies who are actively working to ensure that their business operations are based on sound environmental practices.

2. Click an insertion point between the question mark and the paragraph mark at the end of the *Why was it started?* heading, press Enter, and type the following:

   The chartering of Redmond

There's *Redmond* again; that's the third time we've had to type it. Let's look at a couple of ways we can save keystrokes and ensure that the words and phrases we use repeatedly are always entered correctly.

Using AutoText

We use Word's AutoText feature to store text or a graphic so that we can later retrieve it by typing its name and pressing the F3 key. For this example, we'll turn a word we have already typed into an AutoText entry. Follow along as we simplify the typing of *Redmond*:

1. Select *Redmond,* the word you just typed, and choose AutoText from the Edit menu to display this dialog box:

2. Type *red* in the Name edit box and click the Add button. Word closes the dialog box.

Now let's use the entry we've just created as we write a few more paragraphs for the backgrounder:

1. Click an insertion point after *Redmond* in the paragraph that begins *The chartering of Redmond*, type a space, and then type the following (don't press the Spacebar after *red*):

   BEAT was spearheaded by long-time red

2. Press F3. Word replaces *red* with the *Redmond* entry.

3. Continue typing the following paragraph, using the *red-F3* sequence to insert *Redmond* where indicated. Be sure to type the error marked in bold exactly as you see it so that you will have a mistake to correct later in the chapter. Also include the **** characters, which are placeholders for information we'll add later.

   resident William Henry, President of Creative GlassWorks. Struck by the incongruity between his family's efforts to recycle household waste and the fact that his company was sending several dumpsters of garbage to the red-F3 *landfill every month, Henry began looking for other ways to dispose*

*of the packaging in which his company received raw
materials. His questions caused one of his suppliers, ****, to
explore alternative packaging methods. The result was less
garbage in the Creative GlassWorks dumpsters at no
additional cost and negligible other effects for either
company. In the meantime, Henry learned about National
BEAT, and a few months of persuasive* **campaining** *later,*
red-F3 *BEAT became the newest chapter of a rapidly growing
national association.*

Suppose we forget the code for an AutoText entry. Does that
mean we can't use the entry anymore? Not at all. Try this:

1. Click an insertion point at the end of the *How can I find out
   more?* heading, press Enter, and type *Come to a meeting*
   followed by a period and a space.

2. Choose AutoText from the Edit menu to see this dialog box:

   The name in the list box serves as a reminder of the entry we
   have created. If we create more than one entry, we can select
   them in turn and check the Preview box to see what each one
   represents.

3. With *red* selected in the list, click the Insert button. Word closes
   the dialog box and inserts the entry *Redmond* at the insertion
   point.

4. Finish typing the paragraph as follows:

   *BEAT meets at 8:00 AM on the last Tuesday of every month
   in the Community Center.*

Now that we've simplified the typing of the word *Redmond*, you've probably noticed some other words that could benefit from the same treatment. How about *National BEAT* and *Redmond BEAT*? To simplify the typing of these entries, we'll use AutoCorrect.

Using AutoCorrect

We use the AutoCorrect feature when we want Word to automatically replace a name with its entry. AutoCorrect names should be unique sequences of characters that we are not likely to use normally in a document. Try this:

1. In the backgrounder's first heading, select *Redmond BEAT* and then choose AutoCorrect from the Tools menu to display this dialog box:

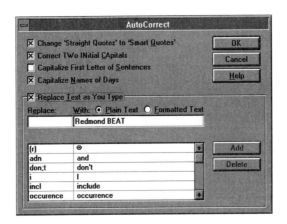

AutoCorrect options

In the AutoCorrect dialog box are several options that take care of common typing "errors." Word can change straight quotation marks (") to open (") and close (") quotation marks, correct two initial capital letters in a word, correct sentences that don't begin with a capital letter, and capitalize the days of the week. You can turn any of these options on or off by clicking the corresponding check box.

Word is waiting for you to enter the name you want Word to replace with the selected text, which appears in the With edit box. At the bottom of the AutoCorrect dialog box is a ready-made list of "words" that Word replaces each time you type them.

2. In the Replace edit box, type *rb* as the name of the entry and click Add. Word adds the name and its replacement to the list.

3. Type *nb* in the Replace edit box, double-click *Redmond* in the With edit box to select it, and type *National* and a space. The entry in the With edit box is now *National BEAT*. Click Add and then click OK to close the dialog box.

Now let's use these AutoCorrect entries so that you can get a feel for what time-savers they can be:

1. Click an insertion point at the end of the *When was it started?* heading, press Enter, and type this:

   nb, *which currently has **** local chapters, was founded in 1987.* rb *was founded in 1990.*

2. Next, click an insertion point at the end of the *Who can join?* heading, press Enter, and type the following (be sure to misspell *the* as *teh*):

   Membership in rb *is open to all companies licensed to do business in* teh *city of* red-F3. *For more information, contact Ted Lee at 555-6789.*

Word Editing Techniques

In Chapter 1, we covered editing techniques that are common to all the Office applications, and you may have already done some simple editing in this chapter if you typed any words incorrectly. In this section, we briefly cover some more ways of revising documents. We'll make a few changes to the backgrounder to get a feel for what's involved.

Deleting and Replacing Text

Word provides a few techniques for deleting and replacing text in addition to those covered in Chapter 1. We'll learn these Word-specific techniques as we add a new paragraph to the backgrounder:

1. Click an insertion point at the end of the *Why should my company join?* heading, press Enter, and type the following (including the error in bold and the AutoCorrect names, which are not italicized):

   Current members cite two main reasons for joining. Many companies are managed by people who were first attracted to this area by its natural beauty adn *who therefore want to be part of* teh *effort to preserve it. Other companies stress* teh *potential advantages in today's competitive markets of being perceived as a "green" company by consumers who are increasingly* **environmently** *aware.*

Smart editing

When you cut or copy and paste text, Word intuits where spaces are needed for the text to make sense. For example, it removes spaces before and adds spaces after punctuation marks. You can tell Word to leave these kinds of adjustments to you by choosing Options from the Tools menu, clicking the Edit tab, clicking the Use Smart Cut And Paste option to deselect it, and clicking OK.

Deleting a word to the left

2. Click an insertion point after the last *e* in *therefore* and then press Ctrl+Backspace to delete the word to the left of the insertion point.

Deleting a word to the right

3. Then click an insertion point to the left of the *f* in *first* and press Ctrl+Delete to delete the word to the right of the insertion point.

Insert mode

As you have seen, Word is by default in Insert mode, meaning that when we click an insertion point and begin typing, the characters we enter are inserted to the left of the insertion point, pushing any existing text to the right. Word can also operate in Overtype mode, meaning that when we click an insertion point and begin typing, each character we enter replaces an existing character.

Overtype mode

Let's experiment a bit with overtyping. Suppose Redmond BEAT was actually founded in 1989, not 1990. Here's how to make this simple correction:

1. Click an insertion point between the first and second 9s of 1990 under the *When was it started?* heading.

Turning on overtype

2. Press the Insert (Ins) key. The letters *OVR* are highlighted in the status bar to indicate that you are now in Overtype mode.

3. Type *8*, which overtypes the second 9, and then type *9*, which overtypes the 0, so that the entry now correctly reads *1989*.

Turning off overtype

4. Press the Insert key to turn off Overtype mode. This step is important; you might overtype valuable information if you forget it.

Moving and Copying Text

We can move any amount of text within the same document or to a different document. Move operations can either be carried out using the Cut and Paste buttons as discussed in Chapter 1 or by using a mouse technique called *drag-and-drop editing*. Generally, we use drag-and-drop editing when moving text short

Drag-and-drop editing

distances; that is, when the text we're moving and the place we're moving it to can be viewed simultaneously. Try this:

1. Select the sentence that begins *National BEAT* under the *When was it started?* heading, including the space after the period.

2. Point to the highlighted text, hold down the left mouse button, drag the shadow insertion point after the period following 1989, and release the mouse button. The selected text moves to the specified location. You have, in effect, transposed the two sentences in this paragraph.

Moving text with drag-and-drop editing

3. Now select the *When was it started?* heading and the following paragraph and move them above the *Why was it started?* heading.

The procedure for copying text is similar to that for moving text. Try copying some text with the drag-and-drop technique:

1. Use the vertical scroll bar to position the backgrounder on the screen so that both the *Who can join?* and *How can I find out more?* sections are visible at the same time.

2. Click an insertion point at the beginning of the sentence that reads *For more information* under the *Who can join?* heading.

3. Select the sentence by holding down Ctrl and Shift simultaneously and then pressing the Right Arrow key until you have selected the entire sentence.

4. Point to the selected text, hold down the left mouse button, and drag the shadow insertion point to the right of the last period in the document (after *Community Center*). While still holding down the mouse button, hold down the Ctrl key (a small plus sign appears next to the mouse pointer), and then release the key and the mouse button together. Immediately, a copy of the selected sentence appears in the location designated by the shadow insertion point, as shown on the next page.

Copying text with drag-and-drop editing

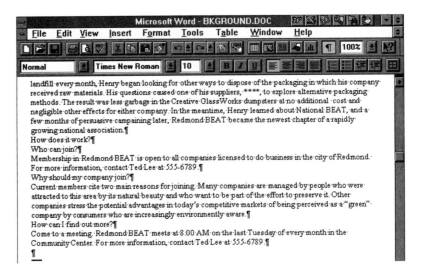

5. Now select the first instance of the *For more information* sentence and press Delete.

Organizing Documents

You have seen how to move text around in a document using cut-and-paste and drag-and-drop editing, but when a document has headings as well as ordinary text, it's often simpler to use Word's Outlining feature to move things around. Most people are accustomed to thinking of outlining as the process that precedes the writing of lengthy documents. With Word, however, outlining is not a separate process but simply another way of looking at a document. Once we use Word's Outlining feature with a particular document, we can switch to outline view at any time to get an overview of our work. In this section, we'll set up the outline for the backgrounder and then use it to reorganize the document. Let's get started:

1. Choose Outline from the View menu. Word displays the Outlining toolbar, which allows you to organize your document by assigning levels to the information on the screen. Because Word considers all the headings and paragraphs of the backgrounder to be ordinary body text, each one is identified in the selection area to its left by a small hollow square.

2. Move the pointer over the Outlining toolbar, using ToolTips to get an idea of what each button does, and then press Ctrl+End to move to the end of the document.

Outlining

Deleting headings

To delete a heading from an outline, select the heading and press Delete. If you want to also delete the heading's subordinate headings and text, collapse the outline before you make your selection. Otherwise, expand the outline before you select the heading so that you can see exactly which paragraphs will be affected when you press Delete.

3. On a new line, type *Redmond Business Environmental Action Team*, and then click the Promote button on the Outlining toolbar. Word moves the heading to the left and makes it bigger to reflect its new status. Notice that Heading 1, the style that Word has applied to the heading, appears in the Style box at the left end of the Formatting toolbar. (See page 66 for more information about styles.) With Word, you can create up to nine heading levels, called Heading 1 through Heading 9. Also notice the large minus icon next to the heading; it indicates that the heading has no subheadings or text.

The Promote button

Heading styles

4. Click an insertion point anywhere in the *How can I find out more?* heading and click the Promote button. Repeat this step for each of the other headings so that they're all the level 1 style.

5. Click the Show Heading 1 button. Word collapses the outline so that only the level 1 headings are visible:

The Show Heading 1 button

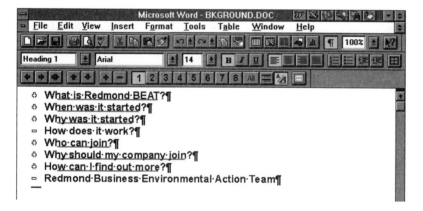

As already mentioned, a minus icon indicates that the heading doesn't have subordinate headings or text; a plus icon indicates that it does. In addition, Word puts a gray underscore below headings whose subordinate information is hidden. Now let's do a little reorganizing:

Outline symbols

6. Click an insertion point in the *Redmond Business Environmental Action Team* heading and click the Move Up button repeatedly until the heading is at the top of the document.

The Move Up button

7. Select both the *When was it started?* and *Why was it started?* headings and then click the Move Down button once to move both headings below the *How does it work?* heading.

The Move Down button

The Expand button

8. Click the Expand button to display the body text below the two selected headings. As you can see here, the paragraphs moved with their headings:

The Collapse button

9. Click the Collapse button to hide the text again.

What happens if we want to add information to the document while we are in outline view? Simple!

1. Click an insertion point at the end of the *How does it work?* heading and press Enter. Word assumes you want to type another level 1 heading.

The Demote To Body Text button

2. Click the Demote To Body Text button on the Outlining toolbar and type the following, including the errors in bold:

*Member companies agree to participate in two ongoing efforts: 1. They pledge to scrutinize their operations and wherever possible, implement procedures that will minimize any adverse **affects** on the environment. 2. They agree to field-test new "**environmently** kind" products and services to evaluate their potential impact on both company costs and the environment.*

3. Click the Show Heading 1 button to display only the headings.

Looking through the outline, notice that all the headings except
the first should really be level 2. You have seen how to use the
Promote button to bump headings up one level. Here's how to
bump them down:

1. Select all the headings except the first and click the Demote
   button on the Outlining toolbar. Word both moves the selected
   headings to the right so that their relationship to the level 1 heading
   above is readily apparent, and changes their formatting. In the
   Style box on the Formatting toolbar, Heading 2 is displayed. The
   minus icon to the left of the first heading changes to a plus icon,
   indicating that it now has subordinate headings and text.

The Demote button

2. Click the Show All button to see these results:

The Show All button

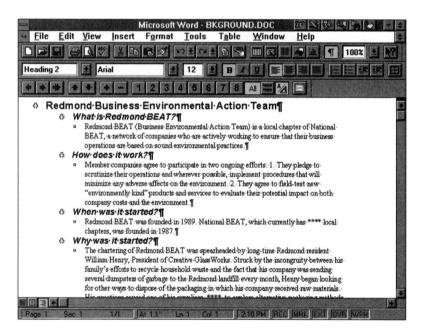

Well, after that brief introduction to Word's Outlining feature,
we'll return to normal view so that we can move on with the rest
of the chapter:

1. Click the Normal View button at the left end of the horizontal
   scroll bar. Having set up the document's outline, you can return
   to outline view at any time by simply clicking the Outline View
   button at the left end of the horizontal scroll bar.

**The Normal View and
Outline View buttons**

2. Click the Save button to save your work.

Finding and Replacing

With Word, we can search a document for specific characters. We can also specify replacement characters. As you'll see if you follow along with the next example, finding a series of characters is easy.

Finding Text

Recall that while typing the Redmond BEAT backgrounder, we left the characters **** as placeholders for information that needed to be added later. Suppose we now need to locate the placeholders so that we can substitute the correct information. In a document as short as the backgrounder, we would have no difficulty locating ****. But if the current document were many pages long and several placeholders were involved, we would probably want to use the Find command to locate them. Follow these steps:

1. Press Ctrl+Home to move the insertion point to the top of the document.

2. Choose Find from the Edit menu. Word displays this dialog box:

3. Enter **** in the Find What edit box.

Editing during a search or replace

You can edit your document in the middle of a search or replace operation without closing the Find or Replace dialog box. Simply click the document window to activate it, make your changes, and then click anywhere in the Find or Replace dialog box to continue your search or replace.

4. Leave the other options as they are and click Find Next. Word searches the document, stopping when it locates the first occurrence of ****.

5. Click Cancel to close the dialog box and then type *210* to replace the highlighted placeholder.

6. Press Shift+F4 to repeat the Find command with the same Find What text and options as the previous search. Word locates the second ****.

7. Replace the selection with *Jordan Manufacturing*.

Most of our searches will be as simple as this one was, but we can also refine our searches by using the options in the Find dialog box and by entering special characters (see the tip on page 44). For example, suppose we regularly confuse the two words *affect* and *effect*. We can check our use of these words in the backgrounder, as follows:

Refining a search

1. Press Ctrl+Home to move to the top of the document. Choose the Find command from the Edit menu, and enter *?ffect* in the Find What edit box. The ? is a *wildcard* character that stands for any single character.

2. Click the arrow to the right of Down and select All as the Search option. Then click Use Pattern Matching to tell Word to look for a string of characters that matches the Find What pattern, and click Find Next to start the search. Word stops at the word *affects* in the second paragraph.

3. This use of *affects* is incorrect, so click Cancel to close the dialog box and change the *a* to *e*.

4. Press Shift+F4 to repeat the search. Word stops at the word *effects*, which is correct.

5. Press Shift+F4 again to ensure that the document contains no other instances of the Find What text, and click No when Word asks whether you want to continue the search.

Replacing Text

Often, we will search a document for a series of characters with the intention of replacing them. When we need to make the same replacement more than a couple of times, using the Replace command automates the process. As an example, let's find all occurrences of *National BEAT* and change them to *USA BEAT*:

1. Press Ctrl+Home to move to the beginning of the document and then choose the Replace command from the Edit menu. Word displays the dialog box shown on the next page.

Finding and replacing formats

To search for text to which you have assigned a particular format, choose Find from the Edit menu, click the Format button, and then click Font for character formats or Paragraph for paragraph formats. In the Find Font or Find Paragraph dialog box, specify the format you want to find, click OK to return to the Find dialog box, and click Find Next. Word highlights the next text entry formatted with that format. You can use the Replace command to change a particular format. For example, to change all bold text to bold italic, choose Replace from the Edit menu, click Format and then Font, click Bold in the Font Style list, and click OK. Then click the Replace With edit box, click Format and then Font, click Bold Italic in the Font Style list, and click OK. Back in the Replace dialog box, click either Find Next and Replace or Replace All, depending on whether you want to confirm the replacement of each case of the specified format.

Notice that the settings from the Find dialog box have been applied to this dialog box and that the Find What text from the previous search is in this dialog box's Find What edit box.

2. Replace the Find What text by typing *National BEAT*.

3. In the Replace With edit box, type *USA BEAT* and press Enter. Word highlights the first occurrence of the Find What text.

4. Click Replace. Word continues the search and highlights the second occurrence.

5. Click Replace All to replace any remaining occurrences and click No when Word asks if you want to continue searching.

6. Click Close to close the Replace dialog box.

As with the Find command, we can use the Match Case, Find Whole Words Only, Use Pattern Matching, and Sounds Like options to refine the replace procedure. (See the adjacent tip for more information.)

Checking Spelling

Nothing detracts from a document like a typo. In the past, your readers might have overlooked the occasional misspelling. These days, running your word processor's spelling checker is so easy that readers tend to be less forgiving. For example, resumes and job-application letters with typos will more often than not end up in the recycling bin. The moral: Get in the habit of spell checking all your documents, especially before distributing printed copies.

As we created the backgrounder in this chapter, we deliberately included a few errors. Now let's see how Word handles the misspellings:

1. With the insertion point located at the top of the backgrounder, click the Spelling button on the toolbar. Word automatically begins checking each word of the document, starting with the word containing the insertion point, against its built-in dictionary. When Word finds a word that is not in its dictionary, it displays this Spelling dialog box:

The Spelling button

2. As you can see, Word stopped at the word *Redmond*. Possible substitutes appear in the Suggestions list, with the closest match to the unrecognized word displayed in the Change To edit box. Since this spelling is correct, click Ignore All so that Word ignores all other occurrences of *Redmond* in the document.

3. Next, Word stops at the word *environmently*. Click the Change All button to tell Word that you want to change all occurrences of this misspelling.

4. Word continues the spelling check, stops at *GlassWorks*, and suggests *glassworks* in the Change To edit box. Click Ignore All to leave all occurrences of this name as they are.

5. Word stops at the word *dumpsters*. Although this term is not in Word's dictionary, it is correct, so click Ignore All again.

6. Next Word stops at *campaining*—a genuine misspelling. Click Change to accept Word's suggestion, *campaigning*. If Word's suggestion is not correct but one of the words in the Suggestions list is the one you want, you can select that word and then click Change. If none of the suggestions is correct, you can type the correction in the Change To edit box and then click Change.

Checking the spelling of a selection

To check the spelling of part of a document or even a single word, select the text or word and then click the Spelling button. Word checks the selection the same way it checks an entire document, and you use the same techniques to ignore or change any words the program does not recognize.

(You can also edit the word directly in the document without closing the Spelling dialog box.)

7. When Word reaches the end of the document, it closes the Spelling dialog box and displays a message that the spelling check is complete. Click OK to return to your document.

Creating and Using Custom Dictionaries

Why use custom dictionaries?

As you have seen, we can tell Word to remember the words it should ignore during a spelling check so that it does not stumble over them if they occur later in the document. If we check the document again during the same Word session, Word won't stop for the words we told it to ignore. However, if we quit Word and check the document in a later session or if we check a different document, Word again stops for those words. That's where custom dictionaries come in handy. We can add names, technical terms, and other nonstandard words that we use frequently to a custom dictionary so that Word no longer flags them every time we perform a spelling check.

Follow these steps to add a few words to CUSTOM.DIC:

1. Save the backgrounder and choose Exit from the File menu to quit Word. Then reload Word, and reopen the backgrounder by choosing it from the bottom of the File menu.

2. Click the Spelling button on the toolbar to begin checking the spelling of the backgrounder.

3. When Word displays *Redmond* in the Spelling dialog box, click the Add button. Once the word is listed in CUSTOM.DIC, Word no longer treats it as a misspelling.

4. When Word stops on *GlassWorks*, click the Add button to add this word to the custom dictionary. Repeat this step for the word *dumpsters*.

5. When Word completes the spelling check, click OK to return to your document.

6. Click the Print button to print the backgrounder. Your document should look like the one shown at the beginning of this chapter.

The Thesaurus

You can use the Word Thesaurus to look up synonyms for a selected word by choosing Thesaurus from the Tools menu. Word displays the Thesaurus dialog box and suggests alternative words for the selected word. To replace the word in your document with one of these alternatives, select the new word in the Meanings list and click the Replace button. You can also select an alternative word and click Look Up to display a list of alternatives for the alternative! Click Cancel to close the Thesaurus dialog box.

If you want, you can create custom dictionaries for different types of documents. To create a dictionary, choose Options from the Tools menu, click the Spelling tab, and click the New button in the Custom Dictionaries section. Type a name for the dictionary and click OK. Before you can use the custom dictionary, you must open it by selecting it in the Custom Dictionaries section of the Options dialog box and clicking OK. Then when you check a document's spelling, you can select the custom dictionary from the Add Words To drop-down list in the Spelling dialog box so that any words you add will be stored in that dictionary, not CUSTOM.DIC.

Using different dictionaries for different types of documents

You can't rely on Word's spelling checker to identify every error in your documents. Errors of grammar, syntax, or improper word usage will slip by in a spelling check as long as the words are spelled correctly. You should always read through your documents to look for any errors that Word might miss.

3

More About Word

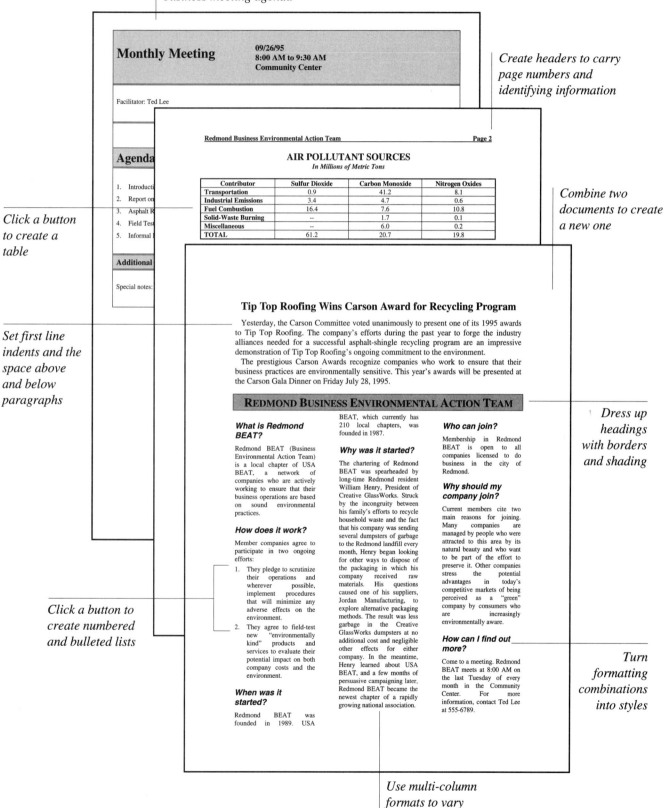

Use Word's Agenda Wizard to create a business meeting agenda

Create headers to carry page numbers and identifying information

Click a button to create a table

Combine two documents to create a new one

Set first line indents and the space above and below paragraphs

Dress up headings with borders and shading

Click a button to create numbered and bulleted lists

Turn formatting combinations into styles

Use multi-column formats to vary document designs

Monthly Meeting

09/26/95
8:00 AM to 9:30 AM
Community Center

Facilitator: Ted Lee

Agenda

1. Introducti
2. Report on
3. Asphalt R
4. Field Test
5. Informal

Additional

Special notes:

Redmond Business Environmental Action Team   Page 2

AIR POLLUTANT SOURCES
In Millions of Metric Tons

Contributor	Sulfur Dioxide	Carbon Monoxide	Nitrogen Oxides
Transportation	0.9	41.2	8.1
Industrial Emissions	3.4	4.7	0.6
Fuel Combustion	16.4	7.6	10.8
Solid-Waste Burning	--	1.7	0.1
Miscellaneous	--	6.0	0.2
TOTAL	61.2	20.7	19.8

Tip Top Roofing Wins Carson Award for Recycling Program

Yesterday, the Carson Committee voted unanimously to present one of its 1995 awards to Tip Top Roofing. The company's efforts during the past year to forge the industry alliances needed for a successful asphalt-shingle recycling program are an impressive demonstration of Tip Top Roofing's ongoing commitment to the environment.

The prestigious Carson Awards recognize companies who work to ensure that their business practices are environmentally sensitive. This year's awards will be presented at the Carson Gala Dinner on Friday July 28, 1995.

REDMOND BUSINESS ENVIRONMENTAL ACTION TEAM

What is Redmond BEAT?

Redmond BEAT (Business Environmental Action Team) is a local chapter of USA BEAT, a network of companies who are actively working to ensure that their business operations are based on sound environmental practices.

How does it work?

Member companies agree to participate in two ongoing efforts:

1. They pledge to scrutinize their operations and wherever possible, implement procedures that will minimize any adverse effects on the environment.
2. They agree to field-test new "environmentally kind" products and services to evaluate their potential impact on both company costs and the environment.

When was it started?

Redmond BEAT was founded in 1989. USA

BEAT, which currently has 210 local chapters, was founded in 1987.

Why was it started?

The chartering of Redmond BEAT was spearheaded by long-time Redmond resident William Henry, President of Creative GlassWorks. Struck by the incongruity between his family's efforts to recycle household waste and the fact that his company was sending several dumpsters of garbage to the Redmond landfill every month, Henry began looking for other ways to dispose of the packaging in which his company received raw materials. His questions caused one of his suppliers, Jordan Manufacturing, to explore alternative packaging methods. The result was less garbage in the Creative GlassWorks dumpsters at no additional cost and negligible other effects for either company. In the meantime, Henry learned about USA BEAT, and a few months of persuasive campaigning later, Redmond BEAT became the newest chapter of a rapidly growing national association.

Who can join?

Membership in Redmond BEAT is open to all companies licensed to do business in the city of Redmond.

Why should my company join?

Current members cite two main reasons for joining. Many companies are managed by people who were attracted to this area by its natural beauty and who want to be part of the effort to preserve it. Other companies stress the potential advantages in today's competitive markets of being perceived as a "green" company by consumers who are increasingly environmentally aware.

How can I find out more?

Come to a meeting. Redmond BEAT meets at 8:00 AM on the last Tuesday of every month in the Community Center. For more information, contact Ted Lee at 555-6789.

C hapter 2 showed you some ways to edit, reorganize, and polish the content of your Word documents. In this chapter, we will explore ways to create useful documents with Word's ready-made templates and wizards. We'll then discuss Word features that can give our documents a really professional look.

Using Word's Templates

Template basics

A Word template is a pattern that includes the information, formatting, and other elements used in a particular type of document. Unless we specify otherwise, all new Word documents are based on the Normal template. Word comes with quite a few other templates that we can use as is or modify; or we can create our own templates (see the tip on page 53).

The TEMPLATE directory

As part of the standard installation procedure for Microsoft Office, a number of sample templates were copied to the directory named MSOFFICE\WINWORD\TEMPLATE. To see a list of these templates and a brief description of each one, follow these steps:

1. Start Word and check that both the ruler (choose Ruler from the View menu) and nonprinting characters (click the Show/Hide ¶ button) are displayed.

The Normal template

Word's Normal template, which is stored in a file called NOR-MAL.DOT in the MSOFFICE\WINWORD\TEMPLATE directory, contains all global styles, AutoText entries, macros, and key/menu assignments predefined by Word or created by you. These global elements are available for all documents you create, no matter which template they are based on. If you mess up your NORMAL.DOT file, you can restore the original file by deleting the current version of NORMAL.DOT or by renaming it. Word then creates a new file the next time you start the program. (Of course, you lose any global elements you added to the old NORMAL.DOT.)

2. Choose New from the File menu to display this dialog box:

If the sample templates are installed on your hard disk, the Template list offers a variety of templates on which to base the new document. The default selection (which is available even when the sample templates have not been installed) is Normal.

3. Click the Agenda Wizard once to highlight it. The Description box at the bottom of the dialog box displays a short description of the highlighted item.

4. Press the Down Arrow key to scroll down through the list, reading the description of each item. As you can tell from their names and descriptions, the sample templates provide the basis for many common business documents.

5. When you are ready, highlight Presrel1, and either press Enter or click OK. Instead of the usual blank document, Word displays this press release form on your screen:

As you can see, all the common elements of a press release have placeholders within square brackets, and Word has entered the current date (using the date stored in your computer—see the adjacent tip). Let's fill in the press release now:

1. Select *[Company Name]* (but not the paragraph mark) and then replace it by typing *Redmond BEAT*. (If you ax a paragraph mark by mistake, click the Undo button on the toolbar immediately to reinstate it.)

2. Replace *[Street Address]* with *14000 Leary Way, Suite 100*, and replace the placeholders for the city, state, and Zip code with *Redmond, WA 98052*.

Date fields

Word automatically enters the date stored by your system's clock/calendar when you open a document based on the press release template. Why? Because the document contains a special code called a *field*. Fields can contain a variety of information; this particular field is an instruction to get the current date and display it in the field's location. If you do nothing to this field, Word will insert the current date each time you print the document. If you want to "freeze" the current date, click the field to select it, and then press Ctrl+Shift+F9. The field is converted to normal text that will not be updated and that can be edited. To insert a date field in your document, choose Date And Time from the Insert menu, and in the Date And Time dialog box, select a date format, click the Insert As Field option to select it, and then click OK.

3. Replace *[Title]* with *Tip Top Roofing Wins Carson Award for Recycling Program* and then delete both *[Subtitle]* and its paragraph mark.

4. Replace *[Name]* with *Ted Lee*, *[Company Name]* with *Redmond BEAT*, and *[Phone Number]* with *555-6789*.

Take a moment to admire your work. Without adding any formatting of your own, you've created a professional-looking header for a press release. But that title could use some fine-tuning. It would be better balanced if the line break occurred after *Award* instead of after *for*. Let's fix that now:

1. Click an insertion point to the left of *for*, and press Enter. Oops! That doesn't look so good. You need a way of breaking the line without adding all that extra space.

2. Click the Undo button (the button itself, not the arrow).

Inserting a line break → 3. Now hold down the Shift key and press Enter. That's better:

Why pressing Enter inserts so much space

Pressing Enter to break the title into two lines creates a new paragraph that has all the formatting of the original paragraph, including space above it to set it off from the preceding element in the press release. You can adjust the spacing between paragraphs using the Paragraph command on the Format menu. See page 67 for more information.

Pressing Shift+Enter inserts a line break at the insertion point without starting a new paragraph. The line break is indicated on your screen by the broken arrow after *Award*.

4. Choose Save As from the File menu and save the document with the name *pressrel*.

Below the press release header, we need to enter the text of the press release. This information is essentially the same as that contained in the letter we wrote in Chapter 1. The beauty of a word processor like Word is that instead of retyping the information, we can borrow it from the letter and edit it to suit the purpose of the press release. Here's how:

1. Press Ctrl+End to move to the end of the document, press Ctrl+Backspace several times to delete *[Type information here]*, and replace *[City]* with *Redmond*. (Be sure to leave the dash in place.)

2. Now click the Open button on the toolbar, and in the Open dialog box, double-click AWARD2.DOC to open the letter from Chapter 1 in its own window.

3. Select just the two paragraphs of the letter, including the paragraph mark between them, and click the Copy button.

4. Choose PRESSREL.DOC from the bottom of the Window menu and click an insertion point between the dash and the paragraph mark after *Redmond*.

5. Click the Paste button. The press release now looks like this:

6. Edit the text of the press release so that it looks like the one shown on the next page.

Creating custom templates

You can save any document as a template and then open a new document based on that template every time you need to create that type of document. To save one of your files as a template, choose Save As from the File menu. Click the down arrow to the right of the Save File As Type edit box, and select Document Template. Word displays the list of files stored in the MSOFFICE\WINWORD\TEMPLATE directory. Assign a name to the template with the DOT extension, indicating the file is a template, and click OK. To utilize the new template, you simply choose New from the File menu and select your template to open it, just as you would with any of Word's default templates.

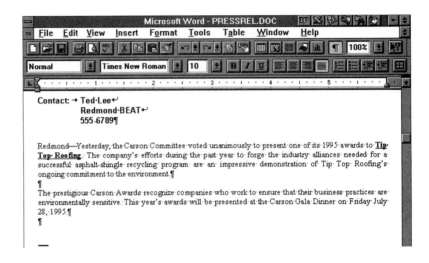

7. Print and save the document, and then close it.

8. Close AWARD2.DOC, clicking No if Word asks whether to save changes.

Using Word's Wizards

When we create a new document based on a wizard, the document we see depends on our answers to questions the wizard asks. Let's use the Agenda Wizard to create an agenda for Redmond BEAT's monthly meeting:

Creating a meeting agenda

1. Choose New from the File menu and double-click Agenda Wizard in the Template list to display this first dialog box:

2. Click Standard to use a standard agenda format and then click Next to display the second wizard dialog box:

3. Double-click the Date edit box and type *09/26/95*. Then double-click the Starting Time edit box and type *8:00 AM*.

4. Click Next to move to the third wizard dialog box:

5. Type *Monthly Meeting* as the title and *Community Center* as the location and click Next to display this dialog box:

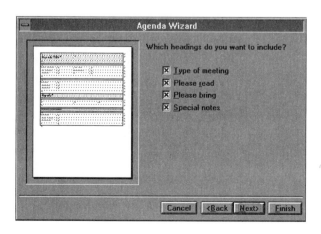

Wizards

Wizards are tools that are incorporated into all of the Office applications to help you accomplish specific tasks. They work in the same basic way, regardless of the task or the application. They all consist of a series of dialog boxes that ask you to provide information or select from various options. You move from box to box by clicking the Next button, and you can move back to an earlier box by clicking the Back button. Clicking Cancel cancels the entire procedure.

6. You can select as many of these options as you want. For this example, deselect all the options except the Special Notes option by clicking their check boxes, and then click Next.

7. Deselect all the options except the Facilitator option in the next dialog box and then click Next to display this dialog box:

8. Double-click the first Agenda Topic edit box to select it and then type *Introductions*. Press the Tab key to move to the Person Responsible edit box and type *Ted Lee*. Press Tab again and type *5* in the Minutes Allocated edit box.

9. Press Tab and type the following information to fill in the edit boxes numbered 2 through 5 and then click the Next button:

Report on Carson Awards	*Sandra Peters*	*15*
Asphalt Recycling Program	*Ima Houseman*	*20*
Field Testing Reports	*William Henry*	
	and Others	*30*
Informal Discussions	*Everyone*	*20*

10. Click Next to confirm the topics, and in the next dialog box, click No and then Next to skip the minutes form.

11. Finally, click Finish to display the agenda, as shown here:

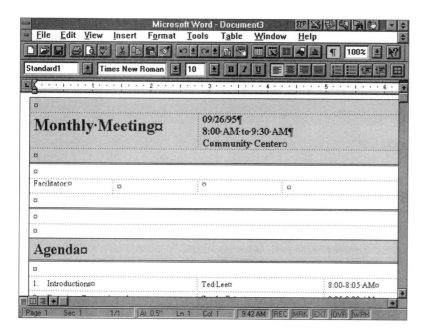

Now add one custom touch:

1. Click an insertion point after Facilitator: and type a space followed by *Ted Lee*.

2. Save the agenda with the name *09-26-95* and then print and close it.

More About Formatting

As you saw in the previous chapter, a well-designed document uses formatting to provide visual cues about its structure. For example, a report might use large bold type for first-level headings and smaller bold type for second-level headings. Summary paragraphs might be indented and italic. In this section, we'll explore some more formatting techniques as we combine the backgrounder from Chapter 2 and the press release we created earlier in this chapter to make a flyer. Follow these steps:

1. Starting with a blank screen, click the Open button on the Standard toolbar. In the File Name list in the Open dialog box, double-click BKGROUND.DOC to open it.

2. To safeguard the original backgrounder file, choose Save As from the File menu and change the name of the version now on your screen to FLYER.DOC.

Painting formats

If you want to format a block of text with a set of formats that you have already applied to another block of text, you can copy all the formatting in a simple three-step procedure. Select the text whose formats you want to copy, click the Format Painter button on the Standard toolbar, and then select the text you want to format. Word duplicates the formatting for the new selection.

Merging documents

3. Press Ctrl+Home to be sure that the insertion point is at the top of the document, and choose File from the Insert menu to display the File dialog box.

4. Select PRESSREL.DOC from the File Name list and click OK to merge the file with FLYER.DOC.

5. Press Ctrl+Home to move to the top of the combined document, and select and delete everything from the press release except the title and the two paragraphs (don't forget to delete the two blank paragraphs). Also select and delete *Redmond* and the dash at the beginning of the first paragraph.

6. Click the Save button on the toolbar to save the combined document, which should look like the one shown here:

From now on, we won't tell you when to save the flyer, but you should do so at regular intervals to safeguard your work.

Making Titles Stand Out

As you know, we apply character formatting when we want to change the appearance of individual characters. Here we'll focus on the titles of the two "articles" in the new flyer. Let's get started:

1. Move to the top of the document, select the title of the press release, change the font to Times New Roman, and change the size to 16 points. Then delete the line break so that the title is all on one line.

2. Now select *Redmond Business Environmental Action Team*, the title of the backgrounder. Click the Center button on the Formatting toolbar to center the title and then change the font to Times New Roman and the size to 18 points.

3. With the title still selected, choose Font from the Format menu. Word displays the dialog box shown here:

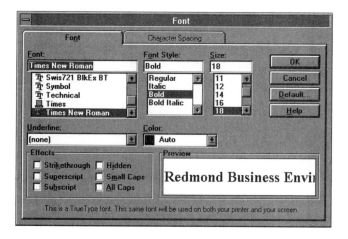

As you can see, the dialog box reflects the character formatting of the selected title. It also provides several formatting options not available on the Formatting toolbar.

4. Click Small Caps in the Effects section to format the title in small capital letters with large initial capital letters and then click OK.

If you want, you can experiment with some of the other options in the Font dialog box before moving on.

Adding Borders and Shading

To emphasize particular paragraphs, we can draw lines above and below or to the left and right of them, or we can surround the paragraphs with different styles of boxes. Let's box the backgrounder title by following the steps on the next page.

The Borders button

The Outside Border button

Changing line styles

Adding shading

1. Click the Borders button on the Formatting toolbar to display the Borders toolbar between the Formatting toolbar and the ruler. (You might want to take a moment to use ToolTips to display the names and descriptions of the buttons on this toolbar.)

2. With the backgrounder title selected, click the Outside Border button. Word draws a box around the title.

3. Click the arrow to the right of the Line Style box and select the 1 1/2 pt single-line option.

4. Next click the arrow to the right of the Shading box and select 25% to fill the box around the title with a light gray color.

5. Click anywhere to remove the highlighting to see this:

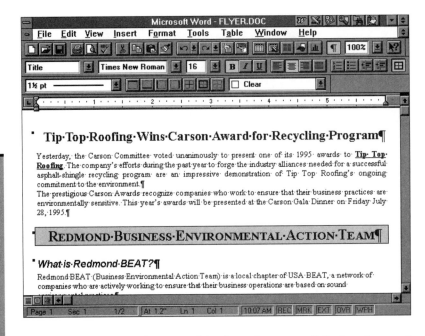

Document sections

When applying different formatting, such as different numbers of columns or different margins, to only part of a document, Word designates the beginning and end of that part with section breaks. You can insert section breaks manually by choosing Break from the Insert menu, selecting an option in the Section Breaks section, and then clicking OK. You can have the new section start at the top of the next new page, at the top of the next even page, or at the top of the next odd page; or you can have the new section continue immediately after the old section.

6. If you want, experiment with the other possible border and shading options. Then click the Borders button to turn off the Borders toolbar.

Setting Up Multiple Columns

Newsletters and flyers often feature multicolumn layouts like those of magazines and newspapers. These layouts give us more flexibility when it comes to the placement of elements on the page, and they are often visually more interesting than single-column layouts. With Word, setting up multiple columns for an entire document couldn't be easier. We simply click the Columns button on the toolbar and select the number of columns we want. And as you'll see if you follow these steps, when we want only part of a document to have a multicolumn layout, we select that part of the document before clicking the Columns button:

1. Select the text from *What is Redmond BEAT?* to the period following the telephone number in the very last sentence.

2. Click the Columns button. Word drops down this grid of columns:

The Columns button

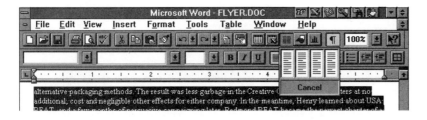

3. Point to the first column, hold down the mouse button, drag across the second and third columns and release the mouse button. Word puts a section break (a double dotted line with *End of Section* at its center) at the beginning of the selected text and another at the end, and reformats the text so that it snakes across the page in three columns. However, because you are in normal view, you see only one skinny column on the left side of your screen.

Creating a three-column layout

4. Click anywhere to remove the highlight and then click the Print Preview button to see the results.

5. Now let's look at the document in page layout view, a cross between print preview and normal view that allows you to see the layout of your document at a size that allows efficient editing and formatting. Click the Page Layout View button at the left end of the horizontal scroll bar, and then scroll until the *RED-MOND BUSINESS ENVIRONMENTAL ACTION TEAM* title is at the top of the window, which now looks something like the one shown on the top of the next page.

The Page Layout View button

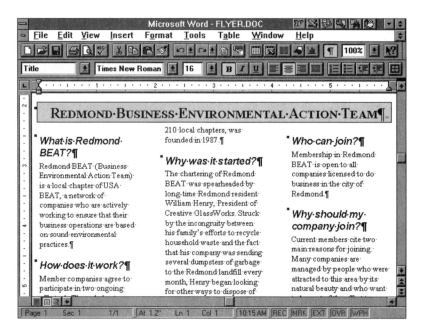

Creating Lists

The second paragraph of the backgrounder contains two numbered items that would stand out better if they were set up in a list format. Word has two built-in list formats: one for numbered lists and one for bulleted lists. Here's how to implement the numbered list format (the bulleted list format works the same way—see the tip on the facing page for more information):

1. Use the vertical scroll bar to move to the second paragraph, click an insertion point to the left of the number 1, and press Enter.

2. Click an insertion point to the left of the number 2 and press Enter. The numbered items now appear in their own paragraphs.

The Numbering button

3. Select the new paragraphs and click the Numbering button on the Formatting toolbar. Word has given the paragraphs a hanging-indent format. (If they were not already numbered, Word would number them too.)

4. Remove the highlight to see these results:

Adding Headers and Footers

The flyer is currently only one page long. For documents that are longer than one page, we'll usually want to add a header or footer, so we'll show you how to do that next.

Headers are printed in the top margin of the page, and footers are printed in the bottom margin. With Word, we have many header and footer options. For example, we can create identical headers and footers for every page, a different header and footer for the first page, different headers and footers for left (even) pages and right (odd) pages, or different headers and footers for each section of a document.

Header and footer options

Suppose we want a header to appear on all pages of the flyer except the first. To create this type of header, we need to add at least one more page to the flyer, like this:

1. Press Ctrl+End to move to the end of the document, and then choose Break from the Insert menu to display this dialog box:

Bulleted lists

To create a bulleted list, you select the paragraphs you want to be bulleted and click the Bullets button on the Formatting toolbar. By default, Word precedes each paragraph with a large, round dot. You can change the bullet symbol by choosing Bullets And Numbering from the Format menu and selecting one of five other standard symbols. You can modify the format of bulleted paragraphs the same way you modify numbered paragraphs.

2. Accept the default Page Break option by clicking OK.

3. Now insert another page break using a different method: Press Ctrl+Enter. Your document has three pages.

4. Press Ctrl+Home to move to the top of the document.

Now let's tackle the header:

1. Choose Header And Footer from the View menu. Word dims the text of the document, outlines the space in which the header will appear with a dotted box, and displays the Header And Footer floating toolbar, as shown here:

The Page Setup button

2. Click the Page Setup button on the Header And Footer toolbar to display the dialog box shown here:

Odd and even

You can create different headers and footers for odd and even pages by selecting the Different Odd And Even option on the Layout tab of the Page Setup dialog box. Word then indicates whether you are creating an odd or even header or footer in the box at the top or bottom of your document. The headers and footers you create using this option are automatically reflected on all odd and even pages of the document.

If necessary, click the Layout tab to display its options.

3. In the Headers And Footers section, select the Different First Page option, and click OK. Word changes the header designation to read *First Page Header - Section 1.*

4. We're going to leave the first page header blank, so click the Show Next button on the Header And Footer toolbar to move to the next page, which begins section 3. (Section 2 is the three-column portion of page 1.)

The Show Next button

5. Click the Same As Previous button to toggle it off, thereby indicating that you want this header to be different from the first one.

The Same As Previous button

6. Now type *Redmond Business Environmental Action Team*, press the Tab key twice, type *Page* and a space, and click the Page Numbers button.

The Page Numbers button

7. Select the entire header and click the Bold and Underline buttons so that the header looks like this:

More about page numbers

If you want your headers or footers to contain nothing but page numbers, you don't have to create a header or footer. You can have Word perform this chore for you. Choose Page Numbers from the Insert menu, and in the Page Numbers dialog box, specify whether the page numbers should appear at the top or bottom of the page, how they should be aligned, and whether a number should appear on the first page, and click OK. Whether you add page numbers this way or by clicking the Page Numbers button on the Header And Footer toolbar, you can format them by clicking the Format button in the Page Numbers dialog box. You can select from five numbering schemes, including Arabic numbers (1, 2, 3), lower-/uppercase letters (a, b, c/A, B, C), and lower-/uppercase Roman numerals (i, ii, iii/I, II, III). You can also specify whether chapter numbers should be included and select a starting number.

8. Click the Close button to return to page layout view and then press Ctrl+Home to move to the beginning of the flyer.

Let's take a quick look at the flyer in print preview:

1. Click the Print Preview button. Then click the Multiple Pages button on the Print Preview toolbar to drop down a grid of "pages" and drag through the left and center "pages" in the top row. Word displays the first two pages of your document side by side, as shown on the next page.

2. Press PageDown to see the third page and then click the Close button on the Print Preview toolbar.

Formatting with Styles

We can work through a document applying formats to headings and other special paragraphs one by one, but Word provides an easier way: We can store custom combinations of formatting by defining the combination as a *style*. We can then apply that combination to a text selection or a paragraph simply by selecting the style from the Style drop-down list on the Formatting toolbar.

Every paragraph we write has a style. When we create a new document based on the Normal template, Word applies the Normal style to all paragraphs unless instructed otherwise. The Normal style formats characters as 10-point regular Times New Roman and paragraphs as single-spaced and left-aligned. When we base a document on a template other than Normal, the styles included as part of that template become available, and as you saw earlier in this chapter, we can then create documents like the press release simply by filling in the paragraphs of the template.

Character styles vs. paragraph styles

Character styles affect only the selected text and apply their formats on top of any paragraph formats applied to the selected text. Paragraph styles affect the entire paragraph containing the insertion point. For example, you can apply a paragraph style that makes the font and size of an entire paragraph 12-point regular Arial and then select the first word and apply a character style that makes the font and size of just that word 18-point bold italic Arial.

Using Word's Predefined Styles

As you know, Word comes with nine predefined heading styles, one for each of the heading levels we can designate when using the Outlining feature. Word also has predefined paragraph styles for a number of other common document elements, such as index entries, headers and footers, and footnotes. However, Word does not list the other predefined styles unless the current document contains the corresponding elements. If we insert one of these elements in the document, Word both applies the style to the element and adds the style name to the Style list. Check this out:

1. Click the arrow to the right of the Style box to drop down the Style list.

2. Scroll through the list. You'll see that Word has added the styles from the press release template, as well as a style for the headers you just created.

3. Press the Esc key to close the list without making any changes.

When Word applies one of its built-in styles to an element, it uses the formatting that has been predefined for that element. Once the style is available on the Style list, we can apply the style to other paragraphs. We can also redefine the style to suit the document we are creating, and we can create entirely new styles.

Creating Custom Styles

Although Word does a good job of anticipating the document elements for which we will need styles, we will often want to come up with styles of our own. For example, the paragraphs of the press release currently have no space between them and no first-line indent, making it hard to tell at a glance where one paragraph ends and another begins. Let's create a style that indents the first line of each paragraph and makes the size of the characters slightly larger:

1. Click an insertion point in the first text paragraph and choose Paragraph from the Format menu to display the dialog box shown on the next page.

The Style dialog box

If styles occur in a particular sequence in a document, you can override the style inheritance rule. Choose Style from the Format menu, select the style you want to modify in the Styles list, and click the Modify button. Click the down arrow in the Style For Following Paragraph box and select a style from the drop-down list to specify the style that will be applied to the next paragraph you create. Also in the Style dialog box, you can click the New button to define a new style, and the Delete button to remove the selected style.

Creating a first-line indent

2. In the Indentation section, select First Line from the Special drop-down list. Word enters *0.5"* in the By edit box as the default first-line indent and shows in the Preview box below how your text will look with this setting.

3. Change the setting in the By edit box to *0.12* and click OK.

4. Now select the entire paragraph and select 12 from the Font Size box on the Formatting toolbar. The results are shown here:

Transferring styles to other documents

Once you have created a style for use in one document, you don't have to recreate it for use in others. You can simply copy the style to the new document. Or if you want the style to become a part of the set of styles available with a particular template, you can copy the style to that template. Simply choose Style from the Format menu, and in the Style dialog box, click the Organizer button. The Styles tab shows a list of styles available in the current document. Select the style you wish to copy and click the Copy button. Word copies the style to the template selected as the Style Available In option.

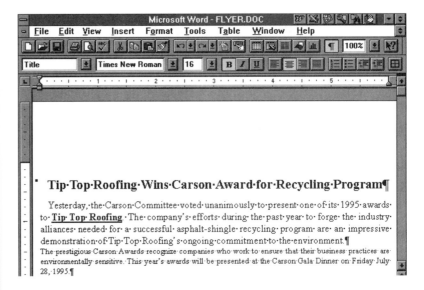

Next, we need to define this particular combination of formatting as a style. Here goes:

1. With the insertion point located in the first paragraph of the press release, click Normal in the Style box to highlight it.

2. Type *Para Indent* (for *indented paragraph*), the name you want to assign to this style. Then press Enter. Word creates the style, adds the style name to the Style list, and displays Para Indent in the Style box to indicate that it is the style applied to the current paragraph.

3. Click an insertion point in the second paragraph of the press release, drop down the Style list, and then select the Para Indent style. Word changes the paragraph from Normal style to Para Indent style.

Now let's turn our attention to the backgrounder part of the flyer. Suppose we want to justify these paragraphs and add a little space before each one. (Paragraphs with space before them are called *open paragraphs*.) Follow these steps:

1. Click an insertion point in the first text paragraph of the backgrounder and choose Paragraph from the Format menu.

2. Select Justified from the Alignment list in the bottom right corner of the Paragraph dialog box. (This is the equivalent of clicking the Justify button on the Formatting toolbar.)

3. In the Spacing section, change the Before setting to *3 pt*, and click OK.

4. Now click Normal in the Style box to highlight it, type *Para Open* as this style's name, and then press Enter.

5. In turn, select each paragraph of the backgrounder (including the numbered paragraphs) and then select Para Open from the Style list to apply that style.

6. Now go back and select the second and third paragraphs under the *How does it work?* heading and click the Numbering button on the Formatting toolbar to apply the numbered-list format "on top of" the Para Open style. The results are shown on the next page.

Applying a style

Modifying styles

To modify one of Word's default styles or one of your own, you first select text using the style you want to change, and then make the formatting changes. To redefine the style with the changes you have made, select the style in the Style list. When Word displays the Reapply Style dialog box, you can select Redefine to modify the existing style or Return to return the paragraph to its original condition. Click Cancel to close the dialog box, leaving your formatting changes intact without redefining the style. Once you redefine the style, all other occurrences of that style in your current document are updated as well.

Now check the layout of the pages:

1. Click the Print Preview button and then press PageDown to view all the pages.

2. If the text from the first page now runs onto the second page, click Close and choose Page Setup from the File menu.

3. On the Margins tab, change Bottom to *0.5*, select Whole Document from the Apply To drop-down list, and then click OK.

4. Check the document in print preview again to verify that all the text now fits on the first page.

Creating Tables

Creating tables in Word is a simple process. We specify the number of columns and rows and then leave it to Word to figure out the initial settings. To demonstrate how easy the process is, we'll add a table to the flyer:

1. Press Ctrl+End to move to the end of the flyer, press Backspace to delete one of the blank pages, and type *AIR POLLUTANT SOURCES* as the table's title, press Enter, type *In Millions of Metric Tons*, and press Enter twice. Make the title bold and 14 points and make the subtitle bold and italic. Center both lines.

Hyphenating a document

By default, Word does not hyphenate your text, but by hyphenating some words, you can really improve the looks of justified columns, such as those in the backgrounder. To hyphenate a document, press Ctrl+Home to move to the top of the document, choose Hyphenate from the Tools menu, and select the Automatically Hyphenate Document option in the Hyphenation dialog box. Click the Hyphenate Words In CAPS option to deselect it so that Word does not hyphenate words in all capital letters, such as BEAT. Then click OK to exit the dialog box. Word quickly hyphenates the document, thus eliminating many of the big spaces between words.

The Insert Table button

2. Press Ctrl+End and click the Insert Table button to drop down a column/row grid.

3. Drag the pointer across four columns and down six rows. The grid expands as you drag beyond its bottom edge, and Word shows the size of the selection below the grid. When you release the mouse button, Word inserts the table structure as shown here:

As you can see, Word has created a table with four equal columns that together span the width of the document's text column. The insertion point is in the first *cell* (the intersection of the first column and the first row). To make an entry in this cell, all we have to do is type, like this:

1. To enter column headings, type *Contributor* in the first cell, and press Tab. The insertion point moves to the cell to the right. Type *Sulfur Dioxide* and press Tab to move to the next cell. Type *Carbon Monoxide* and press Tab. Finally, type *Nitrogen Oxides* and press Tab. (Pressing Tab at the end of the first row moves the insertion point to the first cell in the second row.)

2. Type these entries, pressing Tab to move from cell to cell. (You can also use the Arrow keys or mouse to move around.)

Transportation	*0.9*	*41.2*	*8.1*
Industrial Emissions	*3.4*	*4.7*	*0.6*
Fuel Combustion	*16.4*	*7.6*	*10.8*
Solid-Waste Burning	*--*	*1.7*	*0.1*
Miscellaneous	*--*	*6.0*	*0.2*

3. After typing *0.2*, press Tab. Word adds a new blank row to the table.

Changing column width

You can adjust column widths in three ways: by moving the markers designated with grids on the ruler, by dragging column borders, or by using the Cell Height And Width command. To adjust column width with the ruler, move the pointer over the marker to the left of the column you want to adjust on the ruler. When the pointer changes to a two-headed arrow, drag to the right or left until the column is the width you want it to be. To drag a column border, simply point to the vertical column border, and drag the two-headed pointer to the left or right until it is the desired width. Finally, you can choose Cell Height And Width from the Table menu, where you can enter exact width measurements.

4. Type the following:

TOTAL   61.2   20.7   19.8

5. Click an insertion point anywhere in the first row and choose Select Row from the Table menu. (This menu provides many commands for working with tables. When you have time, you might want to explore it further.) Then click the Center button and the Bold button.

6. Press Home to move to the first cell and choose Select Column from the Table menu to select the first column. Then click the Bold button twice. (The first click turns off the bold style in the first cell.)

7. To center the numbers in their columns, point to the 0.9 entry in the Sulphur Dioxide column, hold down the mouse button, and drag through the numbers to select them. Then click the Center button.

8. Press Home to see these results:

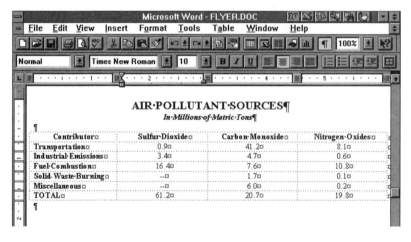

Deleting rows and columns

To delete one or more rows or columns, select the rows or columns, and choose Delete Rows or Delete Columns from the Table menu. (If you don't select rows or columns first, the command is named Delete Cells, and choosing this command displays a dialog box in which you can specify what you want to delete.) To delete the entire table, select the table, and then choose the Delete Rows command.

Before we wrap up this section, let's add gridlines to the cells and put a border around the whole table:

1. With the insertion point anywhere in the table, choose Select Table from the Table menu.

2. Choose Borders And Shading from the Format menu to display the dialog box shown here:

3. In the Presets section, click Grid. In the Line section, check that the 1 1/2 pt single line is selected as the Style setting and then click OK.

Adding gridlines and borders

4. Press Home to see these results:

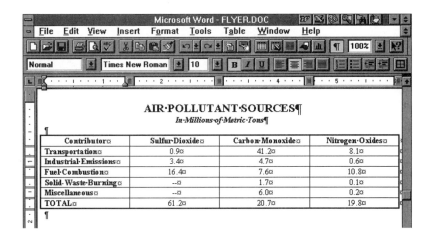

5. Look over the flyer in print preview and then click the Print button. Your flyer should look like the one shown at the beginning of this chapter.

6. Click Close and then save and close FLYER.DOC.

With the features we have explored in these first few chapters, you should have no trouble using Word to create useful documents for your work. If you find that you use Word frequently and would like to explore the program's features in more depth, take a look at *A Quick Course in Word 6 for Windows*, another book in the Quick Course series.

Excel Basics

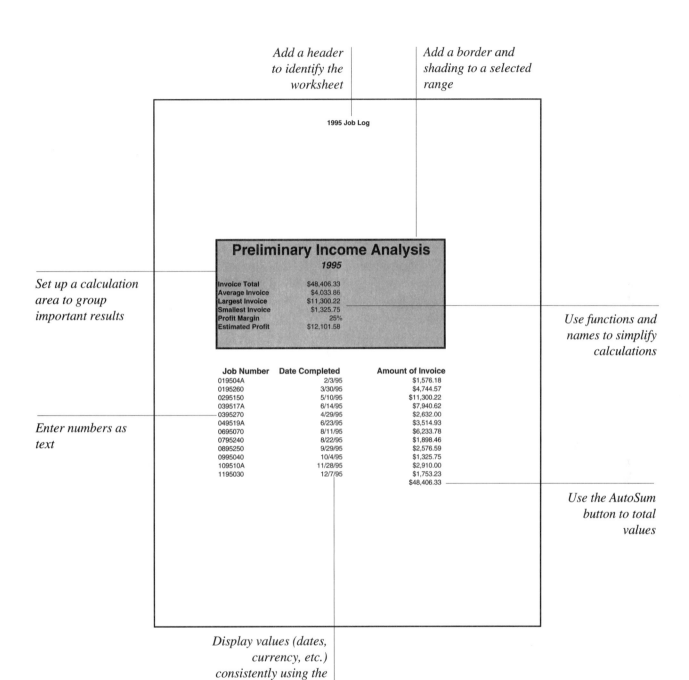

Add a header to identify the worksheet

Add a border and shading to a selected range

1995 Job Log

Preliminary Income Analysis
1995

Invoice Total	$48,406.33
Average Invoice	$4,033.86
Largest Invoice	$11,300.22
Smallest Invoice	$1,325.75
Profit Margin	25%
Estimated Profit	$12,101.58

Set up a calculation area to group important results

Use functions and names to simplify calculations

Job Number	Date Completed	Amount of Invoice
019504A	2/3/95	$1,576.18
0195260	3/30/95	$4,744.57
0295150	5/10/95	$11,300.22
039517A	6/14/95	$7,940.62
0395270	4/29/95	$2,632.00
049519A	6/23/95	$3,514.93
0695070	8/11/95	$6,233.78
0795240	8/22/95	$1,898.46
0895250	9/29/95	$2,576.59
0995040	10/4/95	$1,325.75
109510A	11/28/95	$2,910.00
1195030	12/7/95	$1,753.23
		$48,406.33

Enter numbers as text

Use the AutoSum button to total values

Display values (dates, currency, etc.) consistently using the Cells command

icrosoft Excel, the spreadsheet component of Microsoft Office, is tailor-made for performing calculations on your data. If you want to maintain lists of
information that you can summarize in reports, you should use
Access rather than Excel. But if you need to analyze sales,
calculate budgets, figure out loan or stock information, or compare two financial situations, Excel is the place to be. In this
chapter, we give you an overview of Excel as we create a simple
worksheet. Follow these steps:

The Microsoft Excel button

1. Click the Microsoft Excel button on MOM's toolbar.

2. The first time you start Excel, you are invited to take one of four
   electronic get-acquainted tours. If you're not interested in seeing
   any of these previews, click the Return To Microsoft Excel button in the bottom right corner of the screen. When Excel opens,
   its initial screen looks like this:

Taking up the majority of the screen is a blank *worksheet*, which
as you can see, is laid out in a grid of *columns* and *rows* like the
ledger paper used by accountants. There are 256 columns,
lettered A through IV, and 16,384 rows, numbered 1 through
16384. The rectangle at the junction of each column and row is

called a *cell*. To identify each of the 4 million plus cells on the worksheet, Excel uses an *address*, or *reference*, that consists of the letter at the top of the cell's column and the number at the left end of its row. For example, the reference of the cell in the top left corner of the worksheet is A1. The active cell—the one we're working with—is designated on the worksheet by a heavy border. Excel displays the reference of the active cell in the *name box* at the left end of the formula bar.

Cell addresses

The active cell

An Overview of Workbooks

The worksheet you see on your screen is just one *sheet* in the current file, which is called a *workbook*. By default, each new workbook contains 16 sheets. However, a single workbook file can contain as many as 255 sheets, named Sheet1 through Sheet255. We can have several types of sheets in one workbook, including worksheets; chart sheets, which chart our data; and macro sheets, which store automated ways of manipulating the data or the workbook. This workbook format allows us to store related data on separate sheets but in a single file.

For each sheet in a workbook, Excel displays a *tab*, like a file folder tab, above the status bar at the bottom of the screen. These tabs are handy for moving from sheet to sheet. Let's see how to use them to move around the workbook:

Sheet tabs

1. Click the Sheet2 tab. Excel displays that sheet.

Displaying sheets

2. Next, click the Sheet6 tab. Excel displays Sheet6 and moves the tabs to the left so that the Sheet7 tab is visible.

3. Keep clicking the rightmost tab until Sheet16 is displayed.

An easier way to move between the sheets is to use the *tab scrolling buttons* to the left of the tabs. The two outer buttons take us to the first and last of the displayed tabs, and the two inner buttons move us one tab at a time in the direction of the button's arrow.

1. Click the leftmost button. Excel displays the tabs for the first six sheets but does not change the displayed sheet.

Scrolling tabs

2. Click the rightmost button. Excel displays the last set of tabs, with the tab for Sheet16 still highlighted.

3. Try the other buttons to see how they work and finish by selecting Sheet1.

Although you haven't entered any data in your workbook yet, let's go ahead and save it with the name JOBS95. As you'll see if you follow these steps, saving workbooks is just like saving other Microsoft Office documents:

Saving workbooks

1. Click the Save button. Because you have not yet assigned the workbook a name, Excel displays the Save As dialog box (see page 16).

2. In the File Name edit box, type *jobs95*. Excel will automatically use the extension XLS to indicate that the file is an Excel workbook.

3. In the Directories list, double-click *examples* to indicate that you want to store the new workbook's file in the EXAMPLES subdirectory of the EXCEL directory.

4. Leave the other settings in the dialog box as they are for now and click OK.

Correcting mistakes

If you make a mistake, you can click the cell containing the error and simply type the new entry. If you want to correct part of an entry, click its cell and press F2, or double-click the cell, so that you can edit the entry directly in the cell. You can then press Home or End to move the insertion point to the beginning or end of the entry and press Right Arrow or Left Arrow to move the insertion point forward or backward one character. Press Backspace to delete the character to the left of the insertion point or Delete to delete the character to the right of the insertion point. Then type the correction and click the Confirm button.

5. When the Summary Info dialog box appears, enter *1995 Job Log* in the Title edit box and your name in the Author edit box and then click OK.

From now on, you can save this workbook by simply clicking the Save button.

Entering Data

Most worksheets consist of blocks of text and numbers in table format on which we can perform various calculations. To make our worksheets easy to read, we usually enter text as column and row headings that describe the associated entries. Let's try entering a few headings now:

1. With cell A1 selected, type *Job Number*. As you type, the text appears in both the cell and the formula bar, and a blinking insertion point in the cell tells you where the next character you type will be inserted. A Cancel button (✕), Enter button (✓),

and Function Wizard button (*fx*) appear between the text and name box. Meanwhile, the indicator in the status bar changes from Ready to Enter because the text you have typed will not be recorded in cell A1 until you "enter" it.

2. Click the Enter button to complete the entry. Excel enters the Job Number heading in cell A1, and the indicator changes to Ready. The entry is left-aligned in its cell. (Unless you tell Excel to do otherwise, it always left-aligns text.)

3. Click cell B1 to select it. The reference displayed in the name box changes from A1 to B1.

4. Type *Date Completed*, but instead of clicking the Enter button to enter the heading in the cell, press the Right Arrow key. Excel completes the entry in cell B1 and selects cell C1.

5. Type *Amount of Invoice* and click the Enter button. Here's how the newly entered row of headings looks in the worksheet:

Notice that the headings are too long to fit in their cells. The Job Number and Date Completed headings are still intact, however. (If you're skeptical, click either cell and look at the formula bar.) After we have entered more information, we'll adjust the column widths to accommodate long entries (see page 88).

Long text entries

Entering numeric values is just as easy as entering text. Follow along with the next few steps to enter the amount of each completed roofing job in column C:

Entering numbers

1. Click cell C2 to select the first cell in the Amount of Invoice column and type *1576.18*. Press Down Arrow to complete the entry, which Excel right-aligns in its cell.

2. Enter the following amounts in the indicated cells, pressing Down Arrow after each one:

C3	4744.57
C4	11300.22
C5	7940.62
C6	2632.00
C7	35149.30
C8	6233.78
C9	1898.46
C10	2576.59
C11	1325.75
C12	2910.00
C13	1753.23

Long numeric values

Excel allows a long text entry to overflow into an adjacent empty cell and truncates the entry only if the adjacent cell also contains an entry. However, Excel treats a long numeric value differently. If Excel displays pound signs (#) instead of the value you entered, the value is too large to display in the cell. By default, values are displayed in scientific notation, and values with many decimal places might be rounded. For example, if you enter 12345678912345 in a standard width cell (which holds 8.43 characters), Excel displays 1.23E+13 (1.23 times 10 to the 13th power). And if you enter 123456.789 in a standard width cell, Excel displays 123456.8. In both cases, Excel leaves the underlying value unchanged, and you can widen the column to display the value in the format in which you entered it. (Adjusting the width of columns is discussed on page 88.)

Don't worry for now that Excel does not display these values exactly as you entered them.

Entering Numbers as Text

Now we're ready to enter the job numbers in column A. Normally, we want Excel to treat ID numbers as text rather than as values on which we might want to perform calculations. If the "number" includes not only the digits 0 through 9 but also letters and other characters (such as hyphens), Excel recognizes it as text. However, if the number consists of only digits and we want Excel to treat it as text, we have to explicitly tell Excel to do so. Follow these steps to see how Excel treats two types of job numbers:

1. Click cell A2, type *019504A*, and press Down Arrow. This job number consists of digits and a letter, so Excel treats the entry as text and left-aligns it.

2. In cell A3, which is now active, type *0195260* and press Enter (the equivalent of clicking the Enter button). This job number consists of only digits, so Excel treats the entry as a value and right-aligns it. (Note that Excel also removes the first zero.)

How do we tell Excel to treat an entry that consists of only digits as text? We begin the entry with an apostrophe ('). Follow the steps on the facing page:

1. In cell A3, type *'0195260* and press Enter. (When you type the new entry, Excel overwrites the old entry.) Because of the apostrophe, Excel now recognizes the new entry as text.

2. Enter these job numbers as text in the indicated cells, preceding those that end in 0 with an apostrophe:

A4	*'0295150*
A5	*039517A*
A6	*'0395270*
A7	*049519A*
A8	*'0695070*
A9	*'0795240*
A10	*'0895250*
A11	*'0995040*
A12	*109510A*
A13	*'1195030*

Entering Dates and Times

For a date or time to be displayed correctly, we must enter it in a format that Excel recognizes as a date or time. Excel then displays the entry as we want it but stores it as a value so that we can conveniently perform date and time arithmetic (see the tip below). Let's see how Excel handles different date formats:

1. Enter the following dates in the indicated cells, pressing the Down Arrow key after each one:

B2	*Feb 3, 1995*
B3	*3/30/95*
B4	*5/10/95*
B5	*14-June-95*
B6	*Apr 29, 95*
B7	*6/23/95*
B8	*aug 11, 95*
B9	*8/22/95*
B10	*29-Sep-95*
B11	*10-4-95*
B12	*11/28/95*
B13	*December 7, 1995*

Again, don't worry if Excel displays the dates differently from the way you enter them. Later, we'll come back and make sure

Date and time arithmetic

Each date you enter is internally recorded by Excel as a value that represents the number of days that have elapsed between that date and the base date of January 1, 1900, which is assigned the value 1. As a result, you can perform arithmetic with dates—for example, you can have Excel determine whether a payment is past due. Similarly, each time you enter is internally recorded as a decimal value that represents the portion of the day that has elapsed between that time and the base time of 12:00 midnight.

all the dates appear in the same format. As you can see here, we've now completed all the columns of this simple worksheet:

Selecting Ranges

In Chapter 1, we covered some basic techniques for making selections. Here, we need to discuss how to select blocks of cells, called *ranges*. Any rectangular block containing more than one cell is a range. A range can include two cells, an entire row or column, or the entire worksheet. *Range references* consist of the address of the cell in the top left corner of the rectangular block and the address of the cell in the bottom right corner, separated by a colon. For example, A1:B2 identifies the range that consists of cells A1, A2, B1, and B2. Follow these steps to select ranges of various shapes and sizes:

Ranges

Range references

1. Point to cell A1, hold down the left mouse button, and drag diagonally to cell C13 without releasing the button. Notice that the reference in the name box at the left end of the formula bar reads 13Rx3C, which indicates that you are selecting a range of cells 13 rows high by 3 columns wide.

Selecting more than one block

A range can consist of more than one block of cells. To select a multiblock range, select the first range, hold down the Ctrl key, select the next range, and so on.

2. Release the mouse button when A1:C13 is highlighted. As you can see here, cell A1—the cell where you started the selection—is white, indicating that it is the active cell in the range:

Next, try selecting ranges with the keyboard:

1. Select cell B6, hold down the Shift key, press the Right Arrow key once and the Down Arrow key twice, and release the Shift key. The range B6:C8 is selected.

Selecting with the keyboard

2. Press Ctrl+Home to deselect the range and activate cell A1.

Editing Entries

In this section, we briefly cover some simple ways of revising worksheets. Up to now we have been working with one worksheet. In one of the following examples, we will copy data from one worksheet to another in the same workbook. But first let's see how to change individual entries.

Glancing at the Amount of Invoice column in JOBS95.XLS, suppose we notice that the amount in cell C7 should be 3514.93, not 35149.3. To correct the entry without having to retype the whole thing, follow these steps:

1. Double-click cell C7 to select the cell and position an insertion point in the current entry.

2. Point between the 4 and 9 in the cell and click the left mouse button to reposition the insertion point. Then type a period (.).

3. Press the Right Arrow key once and press the Delete key to delete the second period.

4. Press Enter to confirm the corrected entry.

Checking spelling

If your worksheets will be seen by other people, you will probably want to spell check them. You can easily accomplish this task by choosing Spelling from the Tools menu. Excel then performs a spelling check similar to the one Word performs (see page 44). If you don't want to spell check the entire worksheet, select the cells you want to check and then choose the Spelling command.

Copying and Moving Entries

You can copy an entry or group of entries anywhere within the
same worksheet or in a different worksheet using the Copy and
Paste buttons on the Standard toolbar or the Copy and Paste
commands on the Edit menu. Similarly, moving entries is a
simple cut-and-paste operation. Try this:

1. Select A1:C13 and click the Copy button.

2. Click the Sheet2 tab at the bottom of the worksheet window to
   display Sheet2, and with cell A1 selected, click the Paste button.
   Excel faithfully pastes in a copy of the range from Sheet1.
   (Notice that you don't have to select the entire paste area.)

We can also use a simple mouse operation called *AutoFill* to
copy and paste cells. Follow these steps:

Copying with AutoFill

1. With A1:C13 selected in Sheet2, move the pointer to the bottom
   right corner of the selected range.

2. When the pointer changes to a black cross, called the *fill handle*,
   hold down the left mouse button and drag until the outline of
   the selection is over the range D1:F13.

3. Release the mouse button. Excel pastes a copy of the selected
   cells into the designated paste area.

The result of dragging a copy is similar to using the Copy and
Paste buttons or the equivalent commands, except that Excel
doesn't place a copy of the selected range on the Clipboard.
Because dragging requires that we hold down the mouse button,
it's probably best reserved for copying a range a short distance
from the original.

We can also drag a selection to move it. Here's how:

1. Select D1:F13 and point to the right border of the selection.

2. Hold down the left mouse button and drag until the outline of
   the selection is over the range F1:H13.

3. Release the mouse button. Excel moves the entries to their new
   location, like this:

Clearing Cells

Clearing cells is different from cutting entries. Cutting entries assumes we want to move the entries somewhere else, whereas clearing cells simply erases the entries. Try this:

1. Click the column F header on Sheet2—the gray box containing the letter F—to select the entire column and choose Clear from the Edit menu. Excel displays this submenu:

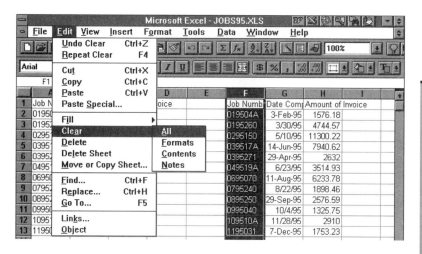

The All option clears both the formats and contents of the cell. Formats clears only the cell contents. Notes clears any notes that you may have attached to the selected cells (see the adjacent tip), leaving the formats and contents intact.

2. Choose All. The entries in the column disappear.

Attaching notes to cells

You might want to attach a note to a cell for a variety of reasons—to explain a formula or remind yourself to check an assumption, for example. Simply select the cell, choose Note from the Insert menu, and type the note in the Text Note edit box. If you want to attach more than one note, click Add, select the next cell, and replace the text of the previous note with that of the new note. When you have finished attaching notes, click OK.

3. Now select A1:H13 and clear the cells by pressing the Delete key. (When you press Delete, Excel leaves any formats and notes intact.)

4. Return to Sheet1 by clicking the Sheet1 tab.

Inserting and Deleting Columns

It is a rare person who can create a worksheet from scratch without ever having to tinker with its design—moving this block of data, changing that heading, or adding or deleting a column here and there. In this section, we'll show you how to insert and delete columns. Follow these steps:

1. Point to the column C header, hold down the left mouse button, and drag across the column D header to select the two columns.

2. Choose Columns from the Insert menu. Excel inserts two blank columns in front of the Amount of Invoice column, one for each column in the selection.

Inserting rows works exactly the same way as inserting columns. You simply select the row headers—the gray boxes containing the row numbers—and choose Rows from the Insert menu (see page 90).

Now let's see how to delete columns:

1. Click the header for column D and choose Delete from the Edit menu. Excel deletes the column and moves the Amount of Invoice column over to take its place, as you can see here:

Inserting and deleting cells

Rather than insert an entire row or column, you can insert a specified number of cells. Simply select a cell or range of cells and choose Cells from the Insert menu. When the Insert dialog box appears, select the Shift Cells Right or Shift Cells Down option and click OK. Excel then inserts the cell(s), shifting the selected cell(s) to the right or down. (Note that you can also insert an entire row above the selection or an entire column to the left of the selection using the last two options in the Insert dialog box.) Deleting cells is similar to inserting them except that you choose the Delete command from the Edit menu and make selections in the Delete dialog box.

You can leave the empty column C where it is for now—we'll use it later.

Formatting Entries

Excel offers a variety of formatting options that let us emphasize parts of a worksheet and display data in different ways. For example, we can use a different font or style to distinguish different categories of information in the worksheet. Try this:

1. Select A1:D1, the range that contains the headings.

2. Click the Bold button and then change the font size to 12.

    As you know, by default Excel left-aligns text and right-aligns values. We can override the default alignment by using the alignment buttons. Here's how:

1. With A1:D1 still selected, click each alignment button, noting its effect.

2. When you're ready, click the Center button, which is a typical choice for headings.

Changing the Display of Numbers

Earlier, we entered dates in column B in a variety of formats. Now we'll show you how to change the date format to reflect the needs of the worksheet. Follow these steps:

1. Use the mouse or keyboard to select the range B2:B13, which contains the dates.

2. Choose Cells from the Format menu to display this dialog box:

AutoFormats

An autoformat is a predefined combination of formatting that works well with certain kinds of worksheets. To apply an autoformat to a worksheet, first choose the AutoFormat command from the Format menu. When the Auto-Format dialog box appears, select an option from the Table Format list (an example of your selection is displayed in the Sample box) and click OK. You can also customize an autoformat by clicking the Options button in the Auto-Format dialog box and selecting or deselecting the options in the Formats To Apply section. It's worth setting up a worksheet and experimenting with autoformats so that you know what is available and which kinds of worksheets can take advantage of this one-stop formatting feature.

3. On the Number tab, select Date in the Category list, select the m/d/yy format in the Format Codes list, and click OK.

Next let's display the column D entries as currency:

Displaying numbers as currency

1. Select D2:D13 and choose Cells from the Format menu to display the Format Cells dialog box.

2. On the Number tab, select Currency in the Category list and then select $#,##0.00_);($#,##0.00) in the Format Codes list to add a dollar sign, a comma, and two decimal places to the entries. (The second set of codes indicates that negative numbers are placed inside parentheses.)

3. Click OK to enter your selection and return to the worksheet.

Changing Column Widths

The entries in column D are now too long to fit in their cells. As a finishing touch for this worksheet, let's adjust the widths of columns A, B, and D so that their entries fit neatly in their cells:

1. Move the mouse pointer to the dividing line between the headers of columns A and B. The pointer shape changes to a vertical bar with two opposing arrows.

2. Hold down the left mouse button and drag to the right until column A is wide enough to display the Job Number heading. Release the mouse button when you think that the heading will fit.

3. Change the width of column B using the same method. Move the mouse pointer between the headers of columns B and C. Then hold down the mouse button and drag to the right until column B is wide enough to display its heading.

Now we'll widen column D using a different method:

1. Select D1 and choose Column and then Width from the Format menu. Excel displays this Column Width dialog box:

Currency vs. accounting formats

Excel provides four currency formats and four accounting formats that are parallel except for the location of the dollar signs in relation to the values. In currency formats, both the dollar sign and the value are right-aligned. In accounting formats, the dollar sign is left-aligned in the cell, and the value is right-aligned. All of these formats consist of two parts; the part preceding the semicolon applies to positive values, and the part following the semicolon applies to negative values. You can quickly apply an accounting format to the data in your worksheet by selecting the data and clicking the Currency button on the Formatting toolbar.

Because you have not adjusted the width of column D before, 8.43—the standard width—is displayed in the Column Width edit box.

2. Type *18* and press Enter. Here's the result:

You can adjust the height of rows the same way you adjust the width of columns. Simply drag the bottom border of the row header up or down or choose Row and then Height from the Format menu to make the row shorter or taller.

Simple Calculations

The whole purpose of building worksheets is to have Excel perform calculations for us. Excel has many powerful functions that are a sort of shorthand for various mathematical, logical, statistical, and financial calculations. However, the majority of worksheets created with Excel involve simple arithmetic.

Doing Arithmetic

In Excel, we begin a *formula* (Excel's term for an *equation*) with an equal sign (=). In the simplest formulas, the equal sign is followed by a set of values separated by +, −, *, or /, such as:

=5+3+2

If we enter this formula in any blank cell in the worksheet, Excel displays the result 10.

Column width shortcuts

To adjust the width of a column to fit its longest entry, select the column and choose Column and then AutoFit Selection from the Format menu, or double-click the column header's right border. To reset a column to the standard width, select the column, choose Column and then Standard Width from the Format menu, and then click OK. To change the standard width, choose Column and then Standard Width, type a new value in the Standard Width edit box, and click OK. (Columns whose widths you have already adjusted retain their custom widths.)

Let's experiment with a few formulas. We'll start by inserting a couple of blank rows:

Inserting multiple rows

1. Select the headers for rows 1 and 2 to select the two rows, and choose Rows from the Insert menu. Excel inserts two blank rows above the table, moving the table down so that it begins in row 3.

Now we're ready to construct a formula in cell A1, using some of the values in the Amount of Invoice column. We tell Excel to use a value simply by clicking the cell that contains it. Follow these steps:

1. Click cell A1 and type an equal sign followed by an opening parenthesis.

Entering cell references in formulas

2. Click cell D4. Excel inserts the reference D4 in cell A1 and the formula bar.

3. Type a plus sign and click cell D5. Excel adds the reference D5 to the formula.

4. Continue to build the formula by typing plus signs and clicking cells D6, D7, and D8.

5. Type a closing parenthesis, type / (the division operator), and then type 5. The formula now looks like this:

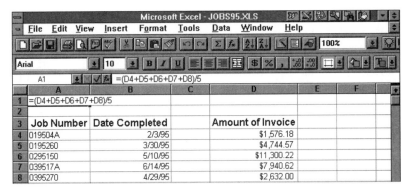

This formula tells Excel to first add the amounts in cells D4, D5, D6, D7, and D8 and then divide the result by 5, to obtain the average of the five amounts.

6. Click the Enter button. Excel displays the result of the formula, 5638.718, in cell A1.

You can use this technique to create any simple formula. Start by typing an equal sign, then enter a value or click the cell that contains the value, type the appropriate arithmetic operator, enter the next value, and so on. Unless you tell Excel to do otherwise, the program performs multiplication and division before addition and subtraction. If you need parts of the formula to be carried out in a different order, use parentheses as we did in this example to override the default order.

Order of precedence

Totaling Columns of Values

Although this method of creating a formula is simple enough, it would be tedious to have to type and click to add a long series of values. Fortunately, Excel automates the addition process with a very useful button: the AutoSum button.

Using the AutoSum Button

The AutoSum button will probably become one of your most often-used Excel buttons. In fact, using this button is so easy that we'll just show you what to do:

1. Click cell D16 and then click the AutoSum button. Excel looks first above and then to the left of the active cell for an adjacent range of values to total. Excel assumes that you want to total the values above D16 and enters the SUM function in cell D16 and in the formula bar. Your worksheet looks as shown here:

The AutoSum button

	A	B	C	D	E	F
1	5638.718					
2						
3	Job Number	Date Completed		Amount of Invoice		
4	019504A	2/3/95		$1,576.18		
5	0195260	3/30/95		$4,744.57		
6	0295150	5/10/95		$11,300.22		
7	039517A	6/14/95		$7,940.62		
8	0395270	4/29/95		$2,632.00		
9	049519A	6/23/95		$3,514.93		
10	0695070	8/11/95		$6,233.78		
11	0795240	8/22/95		$1,898.46		
12	0895250	9/29/95		$2,576.59		
13	0995040	10/4/95		$1,325.75		
14	109510A	11/28/95		$2,910.00		
15	1195030	12/7/95		$1,753.23		
16				=SUM(D4:D15)		

Formula bar: D4 =SUM(D4:D15)

Displaying formulas

By default, Excel displays the results of formulas in cells, not their underlying formulas. To see the actual underlying formulas in the worksheet, choose Options from the Tools menu, display the View options, select Formulas in the Window Options section, and click OK. Excel widens the cells so that you can see the formulas. Simply deselect the Formulas option to redisplay the results.

2. Click the Enter button to enter the formula in cell D16. Excel displays $48,406.33—the sum of the values in D4:D15.

That was easy. The AutoSum button serves us well whenever we want a total to appear at the bottom of a column or to the right of a row of values. But what if we want the total to appear elsewhere on the worksheet? Knowing how to create SUM functions from scratch gives us more flexibility.

Using the SUM Function

Let's go back and dissect the SUM function that Excel inserted in cell D16 when we clicked the AutoSum button so that we can examine the function's components.

With cell D16 selected, you can see the following entry in the formula bar:

=SUM(D4:D15)

Like all formulas, the SUM function begins with an equal sign (=). Next comes the function name in capital letters, followed by a set of parentheses enclosing the reference to the range containing the amounts we want to total. This reference is the SUM function's *argument*. An argument answers questions such as "What?" or "How?" and gives Excel the additional information it needs to perform the function. In the case of SUM, Excel needs only one piece of information—the references of the cells we want to total. As you'll see later, Excel might need several pieces of information to carry out other functions, and we enter an argument for each piece.

Arguments

Creating a SUM function from scratch is not particularly difficult. For practice, follow these steps:

1. Press Ctrl+Home to move to cell A1 and type this:

=SUM(

When you begin typing, the cell's old value is overwritten.

2. Select D4:D15 on the worksheet in the usual way. Excel inserts the reference D4:D15 after the opening parenthesis.

Function names

When you type a function name, such as SUM, in the formula bar, you don't have to type it in capital letters. Excel capitalizes the function name for you when you complete the entry. If Excel does not respond in this way, you have probably entered the function name incorrectly.

3. Type a closing parenthesis and press Enter. Excel displays in cell A1 the total of the values in the Amount of Invoice column—$48,406.33.

Referencing Formula Cells in Other Formulas

After we create a formula in one cell, we can use its result in other formulas simply by referencing its cell. To see how this works, follow these steps:

1. Select cell B1 and type an equal sign.

2. Click cell A1, which contains the SUM function you just entered, type / (the division operator), and then type *12*.

3. Click the Enter button. Excel displays the result—the average of the invoice amounts—in cell B1. (We discuss an easier way to calculate averages on page 98.)

4. Press the Delete key to erase both the experimental formula and its result from cell B1.

Naming Cells and Ranges

Many of the calculations that we might want to perform on this worksheet—for example, calculating each invoice amount as a percentage of the total invoice amount—will use the total we have calculated in cell A1. We could include a copy of the SUM function now in cell A1 in these other calculations, or we could simply reference cell A1. The latter method seems quick and simple, but what if we subsequently move the formula in A1 to another location? Excel gives us a way to reference this formula no matter where on the worksheet we move it. We can assign the contents of cell A1 a name and then use the name in any calculations that involve the total.

We assign a name by using the Name command on the Insert menu. Follow these steps:

1. Select cell A1 and choose Name and then Define from the Insert menu. Excel displays the dialog box shown on the next page.

Name conventions

Certain rules apply when you name cells or ranges. Although you can use a number within the name, you must start the name with a letter, an underscore, or a backslash. Spaces are not allowed within the name, so you should use underscore characters to represent spaces. For example, you cannot use 1995 as a name, but you can use Totals_1995.

The reference Sheet1$A$1 is displayed in the Refers To edit box. This absolute reference points to cell A1 on Sheet1 of the current workbook. (For an explanation of absolute references, see page 112.)

2. Type *Total* in the Names In Workbook edit box and click OK.

If you look at the name box to the left of the formula bar, you'll see that Excel now refers to the cell by the name you just entered, instead of by the reference A1. You can use either designation in formulas.

To see how Excel uses assigned names, try this:

Using cell names

1. Click cell D16, which currently contains the SUM function you inserted earlier in the chapter.

2. Type *=Total* and then press Enter. The worksheet does not appear to change, but now instead of two SUM functions, the worksheet contains only one. You have told Excel to assign the value of the cell named Total, which contains the SUM function, to cell D16.

We can also assign names to ranges. Let's assign the name Amount to the cells containing amounts in column D:

1. Select D4:D15 and choose Name and then Define from the Insert menu. Notice that the Names In Workbook list now displays Total, the name you assigned earlier.

Jumping to named cells

To move quickly to a named cell, press the F5 key. When Excel displays the Go To dialog box, select the name of the cell you want to move to, and click OK.

2. Replace the name Excel suggests, Amount_of_Invoice, with *Amount* in the Names In Workbook edit box and click OK.

Now let's replace the range reference in the SUM function in cell A1 with the new range name:

1. Click A1 to select it and display its contents in the formula bar.

2. Drag through the D4:D15 reference in the formula bar to highlight it.

3. Click the arrow to the right of the name box to display the list of names assigned to the workbook, as shown here:

Selecting a name from the name list

	Microsoft Excel - JOBS95.XLS					
File Edit View Insert Format Tools Data Window Help						

Arial   10   B I U $ % , 100%

Total   =SUM(D4:D15)

		B	C	D	E	F
Amount						
Total						
2						
3	Job Number	Date Completed		Amount of Invoice		
4	019504A	2/3/95		$1,576.18		
5	0195260	3/30/95		$4,744.57		
6	0295150	5/10/95		$11,300.22		
7	039517A	6/14/95		$7,940.62		
8	0395270	4/29/95		$2,632.00		
9	049519A	6/23/95		$3,514.93		
10	0695070	8/11/95		$6,233.78		
11	0795240	8/22/95		$1,898.46		
12	0895250	9/29/95		$2,576.59		
13	0995040	10/4/95		$1,325.75		
14	109510A	11/28/95		$2,910.00		
15	1195030	12/7/95		$1,753.23		
16				$48,406.33		
17						
18						

Sheet1 Sheet2 Sheet3 Sheet4 Sheet5 Sheet6

Edit

4. Click Amount. Excel replaces the range reference with the assigned name, and the formula now reads *=SUM(Amount)*.

5. Now click the Enter button to redisplay the results of the SUM function in A1.

Efficient Data Display

Usually when we create a worksheet, we are interested not so much in the individual pieces of information as in the results of the calculations we perform on the pieces. So before we discuss other calculations we might want to perform with this worksheet, let's look at ways to format our information to make the results of our calculations stand out from our data. It's a good idea to design worksheets so that the results are easily accessible

Calculation area advantages

Creating a calculation area at the top of your worksheet is a good habit to get into and offers the following advantages:

- You don't have to scroll around looking for the totals and other results.

- You can print just the first page of a worksheet to get a report of the most pertinent information.

- You can easily jump to the calculation area from anywhere on the worksheet by pressing Ctrl+Home to move to cell A1.

and in a predictable location. For these reasons, we leave room in the top left corner of our worksheets for a calculation area.

Let's create an area at the top of Sheet1 of the JOBS95 workbook for a title and a set of calculations. We'll start by freeing up some space at the top of the worksheet:

1. Select A1:D16 and click the Cut button.

2. Select A10 and click the Paste button to move the selection to A10:D25.

Now let's enter a title for the worksheet:

1. In cell A1, type *Preliminary Income Analysis* and click the Enter button.

2. Format the title by clicking the Bold button on the Formatting toolbar, and then clicking 10 in the Font Size box, typing *22*, and pressing Enter. The height of row 1 increases to accommodate the larger font.

3. In cell A2, type *1995* and click the Enter button.

4. Format the subtitle by clicking the Bold and Italic buttons and by selecting 14 from the Font Size list.

The Center Across Columns button

5. To center the titles above the calculation area, select A1:D2 and click the Center Across Columns button. Excel centers the titles over the selected area, but the titles are still stored in cells A1 and A2.

Next, we'll set off the calculation area. With Excel, we can get really fancy, using borders and shading to draw attention to calculation results. Try the following:

Adding a border

1. Select A1:D9 and choose Cells from the Format menu.

2. When the Format Cells dialog box appears, click the Border tab and select Outline in the Border section.

3. In the Style section of the Border tab, select the last option in the column on the left.

4. Finally, click the Patterns tab, select the light gray square in the color palette (the second square from the right in the second row), and click OK. Excel surrounds the calculation area with a heavy border and fills the area with a light gray shade.

Adding shading

Now that we've created a calculation area, let's move the calculation in cell A10. Follow these steps:

1. Select cell A4, type *Invoice Total*, and press Enter.

2. Select cell A10 and use the Cut and Paste buttons to move the formula to cell B4. (We'll show you how to quickly restore the gray shading to cell B4 in a moment.)

Moving formulas

Now let's add another touch:

1. Select A4:A9 and click the Bold button.

Preformatting cells

Why did we tell you to select the empty cells below Invoice Total before applying the Bold style? Try this:

2. Select cell A5, type *Average Invoice*, and click the Enter button. The new heading is bold because you already applied the Bold style to cell A5.

3. Choose Column and then AutoFit Selection from the Format menu to widen column A so that the headings fit within the column. From now on, adjust the column width as necessary to see your work.

We can also save time by applying number formats to empty cells. Here's how:

1. Select B4:B9 and choose Cells from the Format menu.

2. Click the Number tab, select Currency in the Category list, select the third set of codes in the Format Codes list, and click OK. Excel formats the selected cells with a dollar sign, a comma, and two decimal places.

> **Underlying vs. displayed**
>
> After you apply a format, the value displayed in the cell might look different from the value in the formula bar. For example, 345.6789 is displayed in its cell as $345.68 after you apply the Currency format. When performing calculations, Excel uses the value in the formula bar, not the displayed value.

3. To see the Currency format for negative values, select cell B5, type *−1234*, and click the Enter button. As you can see, Excel displays the negative value in parentheses, aligning the value with the positive value above it.

The Format Painter button

4. With cell B5 selected, click the Format Painter button on the Standard toolbar and then click cell B4 to transfer the formatting of B5 to B4.

5. Press Ctrl+Home. Here's the result of all your formatting:

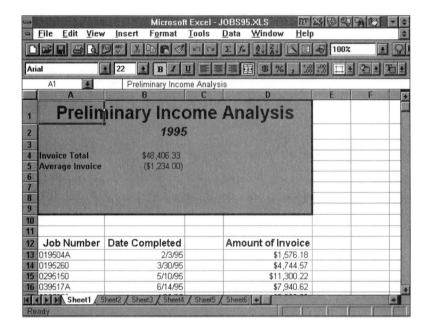

More Calculations

Now let's perform some more calculations on the data in JOBS95.XLS, starting with the average invoice.

Averaging Values

To find the average amount for the invoices we've entered in this worksheet, we'll use Excel's AVERAGE function. We'll use the Function Wizard button on the Standard toolbar to avoid making errors while typing function names, and to make sure we include all the arguments Excel needs to calculate the function. As you'll see, the Function Wizard walks you through the steps of building the formula.

1. Select cell B5 and click the Function Wizard button. Excel displays the first Function Wizard dialog box shown here, which lists the most frequently used functions:

The Function Wizard button

2. Since AVERAGE is already highlighted, click the Next button to display the second dialog box:

The dialog box contains a definition of the function and its arguments. In the Number1 edit box, the insertion point waits for you to enter a number, cell reference, name, formula, or another function.

3. Move the dialog box, if necessary, and then select D13:D24 in the worksheet to add its reference to the formula selection:

Moving dialog boxes

To enter a cell or range reference in an edit box, you can click the cell or select the range on the worksheet. If the dialog box obscures the desired cell or range, simply move the dialog box out of the way by pointing to its title bar, holding down the mouse button, and dragging until you can see the part of the worksheet you're interested in.

4. Click the Finish button to enter the formula in cell B5 and then press Ctrl+Home to see the results. Excel displays $4,033.86 in cell B5.

Identifying Largest and Smallest Invoices

Excel provides two functions that identify the largest and smallest values in a group. To understand the benefits of these functions, imagine that JOBS95.XLS contains data from not 12 but 112 invoices! Let's start with the largest invoice:

1. Select cell A6, type *Largest Invoice*, and press the Right Arrow key to confirm the entry and select cell B6.

2. Click the Function Wizard button and select MAX from the Function Name list. This function gives the maximum value from the range we select.

3. Click the Next button to display the second dialog box.

4. Select D13:D24, click Finish, and press Ctrl+Home. Excel enters the largest invoice amount, $11,300.22, in cell B6.

Now for the formula for the smallest invoice, which we'll type from scratch:

1. Select cell A7, type *Smallest Invoice*, and press Right Arrow.

2. Type *=MIN(D13:D24)* and press Enter. Excel displays the result, $1325.75, in cell B7.

Calculating with Names

The last calculation we'll make with this set of data involves the Invoice Total value from cell B4. As a gross indicator of how well Tip Top Roofing fared in 1995, let's calculate the estimated profit:

1. First insert a couple of new rows in the calculation area by dragging through the headers for rows 8 and 9 and choosing Rows from the Insert menu.

2. In cell A8, type *Profit Margin* and press Right Arrow.

3. Type *20%* and click the Enter button.

A function for every task

Excel has over 320 functions. Many functions are provided for common business and financial tasks—some of them quite complex. To get more information about a function, choose Contents from the Help menu and then select Reference Information. From the list displayed, select Worksheet Functions. Excel displays a list of function information. Select Alphabetical List Of Worksheet Functions to see a list of the functions with brief descriptions of each one.

4. With cell B8 still active, choose Name and then Define from the Insert menu. Excel scans the adjacent cells and suggests the name Profit_Margin. Click OK.

Now for the formula that will calculate the profit margin:

1. Select cell A9, type *Estimated Profit* and press Right Arrow.

2. With cell B9 selected, type the formula *=total*profit_margin* and press Enter. Excel multiplies the value in the cell named Total (B4) by the value in the cell named Profit_Margin (B8) and displays the result, $9,681.27, in cell B9. (Notice that Excel displays the result of the formula in the Currency format. When you inserted two rows earlier, those rows assumed the formatting of the selected rows.)

3. Now select cell B8, type *25%*, and click the Enter button. Instantly, the value in cell B9 changes to reflect the new profit margin, as shown here:

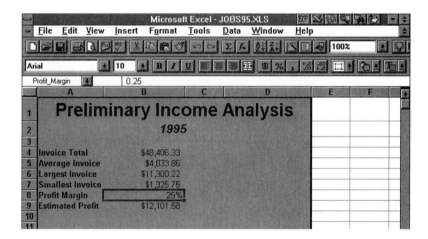

If a hundred calculations throughout the worksheet referenced the cell named Profit_Margin, Excel would adjust all their results to reflect this one change!

Printing Worksheets

Usually, we'll want to preview worksheets before we print them to make sure that single-page documents fit neatly on the page and that multipage documents break in logical places. Follow the steps on the next page to preview the worksheet.

1. Click the Print Preview button on the Standard toolbar. The Print Preview window opens, with a miniature version of the printed worksheet displayed.

2. To examine part of the page in more detail, move the pointer over that part, and when the pointer changes to a magnifying glass, click the mouse button. Excel zooms in on that portion of the page. Click again to zoom out.

By default, Excel prints the worksheet with gridlines around each cell, the workbook's filename as a header at the top of the page, and the page number as a footer at the bottom of the page. For presentation purposes, these default settings don't produce a very attractive printout, so we'll usually want to change them. We make these changes in the Page Setup dialog box, like this:

1. Click the Setup button on the Print Preview toolbar to display the Page Setup dialog box. (When you're not in Print Preview, you can access this dialog box by choosing Page Setup from the File menu.)

2. Click the Header/Footer tab to display the Header/Footer options and then click the Custom Header button to display this Header dialog box:

To add a header, you enter text and codes in the appropriate boxes and click the buttons in the middle of the dialog box. (For a list of header and footer codes, see the tip on this page.)

3. Double-click &[Tab] in the Center Section box and type *&b1995 Job Log*. The &b code tells Excel to print the text in bold.

Header and footer codes

The buttons in the Header and Footer dialog boxes add codes that do the following:

&[Page] Adds current page number
&[Pages] Inserts total number of pages
&[Date] Adds current date
&[Time] Adds current time
&[File] Adds filename
&[Tab]   Adds sheet name

Here are some formatting codes:

&b   Prints following characters in bold
&i   Italicizes following characters
&u   Underlines following characters

You can also format headers and footers by selecting the text you want to format and clicking the Font button (the capital A).

4. Click OK to return to the Header/Footer tab, and then click the arrow at the right end of the Footer option and select (none) from the top of the drop-down list.

Removing footers

5. Now click the Margins tab of the Page Setup dialog box, and in the Center On Page section, click Horizontally and Vertically to center the worksheet horizontally and vertically on the page. The Preview box shows you the effects of your changes.

Centering on the page

6. Finally, click the Sheet tab, deselect the Gridlines check box to turn off that option, and then click OK. The finished product looks like this:

Turning off gridlines

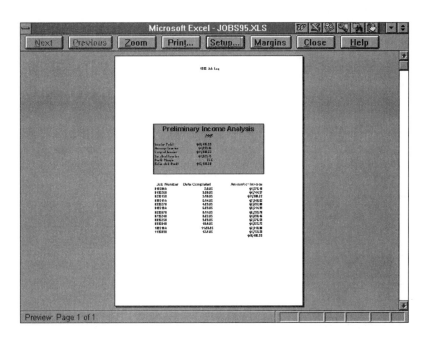

7. When you're ready, click the Print button on the Print Preview toolbar and then click OK in the Print dialog box to print the worksheet.

More About Excel

Consolidate data in a worksheet by category

Change an invoice amount, and links update the other sheets

Link quarterly income amounts to quarterly consolidations

Create an embedded graph that is also linked to the source invoice data

1995 Job Log

Preliminary Income Analysis
1995

Invoice Total	$48,406.33
Average Invoice	$4,033.86
Largest Invoice	$11,300.22
Smallest Invoice	$1,325.75
Profit Margin	25%
Estimated Profit	$12,101.58

Quarterly

Quarter	Total
1	$6,320.75
2	$25,387.77
3	$10,708.37
4	$5,988.98

ted	Quarter	Amount of Invoice
3/95	1	$1,576.18
0/95	1	$4,744.57
0/95	2	$11,300.22
4/95	2	$7,940.62
9/95	2	$2,632.00
3/95	2	$3,514.93
1/95	3	$6,233.78
2/95	3	$1,898.46
9/95	3	$2,576.59
4/95	4	$1,325.75
8/95	4	$2,910.00
7/95	4	$1,753.23
		$48,406.33

1995 INCOME

	1st Quarter	2nd Quarter	3rd Quarter	4th Quarter	Total
Income	$6,320.75	$25,387.77	$10,708.83	$5,988.98	$48,406.33
Expenses	$5,372.64	$21,579.60	$9,102.51	$5,090.63	$41,145.38
Net Income	$948.11	$3,808.17	$1,606.32	$898.35	$7,260.95

We covered a lot of important ground in Chapter 4, and you now have a feel for some of the power of Excel. In this chapter, we introduce you to more Excel techniques, such as how to work with multiple workbooks and how to create a link between two worksheets. We also give you lessons in consolidating and graphing.

Working with Workbooks

In Chapter 4, we copied a range between two worksheets. Excel also allows us to transfer data between two workbooks or compare the information in one workbook with that in another. For example, if Tip Top Roofing kept their 1995 invoice analysis in one workbook and their 1996 invoice analysis in another workbook, they could quickly determine which year was more profitable by simply opening both workbooks side by side on the same screen.

Let's start by opening an existing workbook and a new one:

The New Workbook button

1. Open JOBS95.XLS and then click the New Workbook button. Excel displays a new workbook called Book2.

2. To see both workbooks at the same time, choose Arrange from the Window menu to display this dialog box:

3. Click OK to accept the default Tiled option. Excel arranges Book2 and JOBS95.XLS side by side on your screen.

Copying Entries Between Workbooks

The procedure for copying information between workbooks is the same as for copying between sheets in one workbook (see page 84). Try the following:

1. Activate JOBS95.XLS by clicking its title bar.

Copying sheets

You can copy a sheet within your current workbook or to another workbook. Select the sheet you want to copy and choose Move Or Copy Sheet from the Edit menu. In the To Book edit box of the Move Or Copy dialog box, specify the destination workbook. In the Before Sheet edit box, specify the sheet that will follow the copied sheet. Then select the Create A Copy option and click OK.

2. Select A14:D27 and click the Copy button.

3. Click cell A1 in Sheet1 of Book2 and click the Paste button. Here is the result:

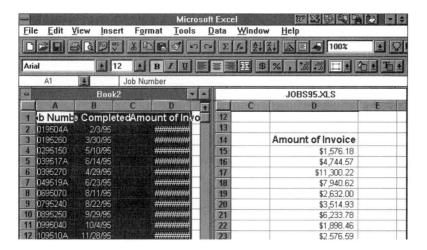

4. Press Ctrl+Home to move to cell A1.

Moving Sheets Between Workbooks

A sheet can easily be moved within a workbook or from one workbook to another. For this example, we'll move a worksheet from Book2 to JOBS95.XLS, but first let's rename a couple of the worksheet tabs so that we can easily identify the worksheet we're going to move:

1. Activate the JOBS95.XLS window and double-click the Sheet1 tab to display the Rename Sheet dialog box:

Renaming sheets

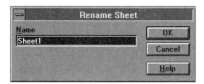

2. Type *Invoices 1995* in the Name edit box and press Enter. Excel displays the new name on the tab.

3. Activate the Book2 window, double-click the Sheet1 tab, and enter *Invoices 1996* as the name.

4. Point to the Invoices 1996 tab and hold down the left mouse button. The pointer is now an arrow with a sheet attached to it.

5. Drag the sheet pointer until it sits between Invoices 1995 and Sheet2 of the JOBS95.XLS workbook. Excel indicates with an arrowhead where it will place the selected sheet.

6. Release the mouse button. The Invoices 1996 sheet now appears in JOBS95.XLS, as shown here:

Deleting Sheets

Before deleting a sheet from a workbook, you should always display it. Excel permanently deletes the sheet, so it is wise to do a quick visual confirmation before sending a sheet into oblivion. In this example, we'll delete the sheet we just moved to JOBS95.XLS and then close Book2. Follow these steps:

1. With the Invoices 1996 sheet active, choose the Delete Sheet command from the Edit menu. Excel warns you that the sheet will be permanently deleted.

2. Click OK. Excel removes the Invoices 1996 sheet from the JOBS95.XLS workbook.

3. Activate Book2 and close it by double-clicking its Control menu icon. When Excel asks whether you want to save your changes to Book2, click No.

Adding sheets to a workbook

You can add a new sheet to a workbook by using the Worksheet command on the Insert menu. Excel inserts the new worksheet in front of the current sheet.

4. Maximize the JOBS95.XLS window, click the Invoices 1995 tab to display its worksheet, and press Ctrl+Home.

Formulas That Make Decisions

There will be times when we want Excel to carry out one task under certain circumstances and another task if those circumstances don't apply. To give this kind of instruction to Excel, we use the IF function.

In its simplest form, the IF function tests the value of a cell and does one thing if the test is positive (true) and another if the test is negative (false). It requires three arguments: the test, the action to perform if the test is true, and the action to perform if the test is false. We supply the arguments one after the other within the function's parentheses, separating them with commas (no spaces). Try this:

How the IF function works

1. Select cell D4, type the following, and then press Enter:

=IF(B4=0,"TRUE","FALSE")

Excel checks whether the value in cell B4 is zero (the test), and because it isn't zero, it ignores TRUE (the action to perform if the test is true) and displays FALSE (the action to perform if the test is false) in cell D4.

2. Double-click cell D4, drag through =0 to highlight it, type *<100000*, and press Enter. The entry in cell D4 instantly changes from FALSE to TRUE because the value in cell B4 is less than one hundred thousand; that is, the test is true.

In this example, the test Excel performed was a simple evaluation of the value in a cell. However, we can also build tests that involve other functions. Suppose that the last character of the job numbers in column A of the worksheet indicates whether the roofing job is a contract (A) or subcontract (0) job, and we want to assign Contract and Subcontract entries to each job number so that we can compare the contributions of the two types of jobs to the Tip Top Roofing income. Follow these steps:

1. Delete the entry in D4. Then insert a new column between columns A and B, and enter the heading *Type of Job* in cell B14.

> **Text values as arguments**
>
> When entering text values as arguments in a formula, you must enclose them in quotation marks. Otherwise, Excel thinks the text is a name and displays the error value #NAME? in the cell. For example,
>
> =RIGHT("Excel",2)
>
> gives the value "el," but
>
> =RIGHT(Excel,2)
>
> results in an error—unless the range name Excel happens to be assigned to a cell or range on the worksheet.

2. Use the Cut, Paste, and Format Painter buttons to restore the entries now in C4:C9 to B4:B9.

3. Select cell B15, type the following, and click the Enter button:

=IF(RIGHT(A15,1)="A","Contract","Subcontract")

You have told Excel to look at the character at the right end of the value in cell A15 and if it is A, to enter *Contract* in cell B15. If it is not A, Excel is to enter *Subcontract*. Here is the result:

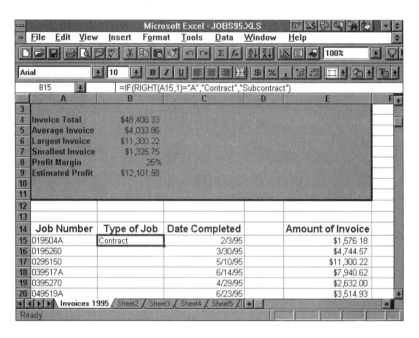

Using Nested IF Functions

When constructing decision-making formulas, we can use IF functions within IF functions. Called *nested functions*, they add another dimension to the complexity of the decisions Excel can make. Here's a quick demonstration:

1. Select cell D14 and enter the column heading *Quarter*.

2. Select column D, choose Cells from the Format menu, and double-click General on the Number tab of the Format Cells dialog box.

3. Now select cell D15 and type this formula all on one line:

=IF(MONTH(C15)<4,1,IF(MONTH(C15)<7,2,
   IF(MONTH(C15)<10,3,4)))

4. Check your typing, paying special attention to all the parentheses, and then click the Enter button.

You have told Excel to check the month component of the date in cell C15. If it is less than 4 (that is, before April), Excel is to display 1 in the corresponding cell in the Quarter column. If the month is not less than 4 but is less than 7 (that is, before July), Excel is to display 2 in the Quarter column. If it is not less than 7 but is less than 10 (that is, before October), Excel is to display 3. Otherwise, Excel is to display 4. If you have typed the formula correctly, Excel enters 1 in cell D15.

Copying Formulas

The IF functions we just entered are arduous to type, even for good typists. Fortunately, we don't have to enter them more than once. By using AutoFill, we can copy the formula into the cells below, like this:

1. Select B15 and position the pointer over the bottom right corner of the cell. The pointer changes to the black fill handle.

2. Hold down the mouse button and drag down to cell B26. Excel copies the formula from B15 into the highlighted cells.

3. Select cell D15, point to the bottom right corner of the cell, hold down the mouse button, and drag down to cell D26. The worksheet now looks like this:

The Fill command

You can use the Fill command to copy entries into a range of adjacent cells. Select the cell whose contents and formats you want to copy, drag through the adjacent range, and choose Fill from the Edit menu. How Excel copies the cell is determined by the command you choose from the Fill submenu. Choosing Down copies the entry down a range; choosing Right copies the entry to the right; and so on. Three related commands are also available on this submenu: Across Worksheets copies entries to the equivalent cells on a group of selected worksheets; Series fills the selection with a series of values or dates; and Justify distributes the contents of the active cell evenly in the cells of the selected range.

4. Select cell B16 and look at the formula in the formula bar. Excel has changed the original formula

=IF(RIGHT(A15,1)="A","Contract","Subcontract")

to

=IF(RIGHT(A16,1)="A","Contract","Subcontract")

Excel changed the reference so that it refers to cell A16 as its argument, not A15. Why?

Relative references

By default, Excel uses *relative references* in its formulas. Relative references refer to cells by their position in relation to the cell containing the formula. So when we copied the formula in cell B15 to cell B16, Excel changed the reference from A15 to A16—the cell in the same row and one column to the left of the cell containing the formula. If we were to copy the formula in cell B15 to E15, Excel would change the reference from A15 to D15 so that the formula would continue to reference the cell in the same relative position.

Absolute references

When we don't want a reference to be copied as a relative reference, as it was in the examples, we need to use an *absolute reference*. Absolute references refer to cells by their fixed position in the worksheet. To make a reference absolute, we add dollar signs before its column letter and row number. For example, to change the reference C4:C9 to an absolute reference, we would enter it as $C$4:$C$9. We could then copy a formula that contained this reference anywhere on the worksheet and it would always refer to the range C4:C9.

Mixed references

References can also be partially relative and partially absolute. For example, $C3 has an absolute column reference and a relative row reference, and C$3 has a relative column reference and an absolute row reference.

Consolidating Data

We can use Excel's Consolidate command to summarize data in a variety of ways. In this section, we'll show you how to use the Consolidate command to total the invoice amounts in JOBS95.XLS by quarter, enter the totals in a separate worksheet, and create a link between the totals and their source data. Follow these steps:

1. First name the destination worksheet by double-clicking the Sheet2 tab in JOBS95.XLS, entering *Quarterly* in the Rename Sheet dialog box, and clicking OK.

2. In cell A1 of the Quarterly sheet, type *Quarter*, and in cell B1, type *Total*. Make the headings bold, size 12, and centered.

Now for the consolidation:

1. Select cell A2 in the Quarterly sheet and choose Consolidate from the Data menu to display this dialog box:

2. Click the Invoices 1995 tab to move to the source worksheet. Excel enters the name of the worksheet in the dialog box.

3. Scroll the Quarter and Amount of Invoice columns into view (if necessary, point to the title bar of the Consolidate dialog box, hold down the mouse button, and drag the dialog box out of the way) and select D15:E26. Excel enters an absolute reference to the selected range in the dialog box.

4. If Sum does not already appear in the Function edit box, select it from the Function drop-down list.

5. In the Use Labels In section, select the Left Column option to tell Excel to use the entries in the Quarter column as labels in the destination worksheet. (Excel returns you to the Quarterly sheet at this point.)

Using existing column labels

6. Select the Create Links To Source Data option to link the data in the Quarterly sheet to the data in the Invoices 1995 sheet and

Linking to the source data

click OK to perform the consolidation. Here are the results after we widen columns A and C:

Outlining worksheets

Excel's outlining feature lets you view as little or as much of a worksheet as you want to see. To outline a worksheet, select all the cells containing data, and choose Group And Outline and then Auto Outline from the Data menu. Excel searches for what it considers to be the most important information (for example, the totals) and uses this information to create different row and column outline levels. Initially, an outlined worksheet displays all its levels. You use the Row Level buttons and Column Level buttons in the top left corner of the window to expand and collapse the outline. For example, clicking the 2 Row Level button displays only the first and second levels and hides any lower levels. You can also click the Hide Detail buttons (marked with minus signs) above and to the left of the worksheet to collapse an outline level. Excel deduces that the last row or column of a section is the "bottom line" of the collapsed section and displays only that row or column. Conversely, you can click the Show Detail buttons (marked with plus signs) to expand collapsed levels. Choose Group And Outline and then Clear Outline to exit outline mode.

As you can see, Excel enters the column labels in the Quarter column and the quarter totals in the Total column, which is now column C. Excel inserted a column and outlined the worksheet to hide the mechanisms used to maintain the link between the totals and their source data. (The topic of outlining is beyond the scope of this book, but if you're interested, you might want to read the adjacent tip.) When you have time, you can practice consolidating data from several worksheets and use some of the other functions available in the Consolidate dialog box. In the meantime, let's use the consolidated quarterly totals in another worksheet.

Setting Up a Summary Income Statement

Before we can move on, we need to set up the following summary income statement for Tip Top Roofing:

Follow these steps:

1. Double-click the Sheet3 tab of JOBS95.XLS and enter *Annual* as the sheet name.

2. In cell A1, type *1995 INCOME*, click the Enter button to enter the title, and click the Bold button to make the title bold.

3. In cell B3, type *1st Quarter* and click the Enter button. Using AutoFill, drag the fill handle to cell E3 (see page 111 and the adjacent tip for more information about AutoFill). Excel fills C3:E3 with the labels 2nd Quarter, 3rd Quarter, and 4th Quarter. Finally, enter *Total* in cell F3.

4. In cell A4, type *Income*.

To link the quarter totals on the Quarterly sheet to those on the Annual sheet, follow these steps:

1. Click the Quarterly tab, select C4 (the first quarter total), and click the Copy button.

2. Click the Annual tab, select B4, and choose Paste Special from the Edit menu to display this dialog box:

3. Be sure the All option is selected in the Paste section and None is selected in the Operation section, and then click the Paste Link button to create a link between the totals in the Quarterly and Annual worksheets.

4. Repeat steps 1 through 3 for the 2nd, 3rd, and 4th Quarter totals in the Annual sheet.

Let's tackle the expenses by following the steps on the next page.

More about AutoFill

You can copy information from one area of your worksheet to another using two methods: Auto-Fill, and copy and paste. These methods produce similar results unless the entry you are copying contains a number that can be incremented, such as in the 1st Quarter heading, or the cell contains an entry from a custom list. If the cell contains a number that can be incremented, using AutoFill copies the entry and increments the number—for example, 1st Quarter becomes 2nd Quarter, 3rd Quarter, and so on. If the cell contains an entry from a custom list, Excel fills the cells with other entries from that list. You define a custom list by choosing Options from the Tools menu, clicking the Custom Lists tab, clicking NEW LIST in the Custom Lists box, and typing the list's entries in the List Entries box. After you click OK, you can enter the list in consecutive cells of any worksheet by typing one of the entries and dragging the fill handle. This feature is invaluable if you frequently create worksheets involving lists of the same entries, such as part numbers or employee names.

1. Enter the following information in the indicated cells:

    A5   *Expenses*
    A7   *Net Income*
    B6   *= .85*B4*

2. Select B4:F7 and assign the Currency format (see page 88).

3. Use AutoFill to copy the formula in cell B5 to C5:E5.

4. Widen column A so that all its labels fit. Then drag through the headers for columns B through F, choose Column and then Width from the Format menu, type *12* in the Column Width edit box, and click OK. All five selected columns take on the new width.

    Now, let's compute the Total column and Net Income row:

1. Select cell F4, click the AutoSum button, and click the Enter button.

2. Use AutoFill to copy the formula in cell F4 to cell F5.

3. In cell B7, type *=B4–B5* and click the Enter button. Excel enters the result, $948.11 as the 1st Quarter's net income.

4. Use AutoFill to copy the formula in cell B7 to C7:F7.

    Voila! Your worksheet should look like the one shown earlier.

Testing Links

Earlier, when we consolidated the quarter totals, we created a link between the Quarterly sheet and the Invoices 1995 sheet. In the previous section, we used the Paste Special command to create a link between the Annual sheet and the Quarterly sheet. With these links in place, we can change the data in the original source worksheet—the Invoices 1995 sheet—and Excel will automatically update the data in the destination worksheets—the Quarterly and Annual sheets. To test the links we created, try the following:

1. Click the Invoices 1995 tab, select E22, type *100000*, and click the Enter button. The total in cell E27 is now $146,507.87.

2. Next click the Quarterly tab and, if necessary, widen Column C. The third quarter total in cell C13 is now $108,810.37.

3. Finally, click the Annual tab and note the changes Excel has made in the summary income statement.

As you can see, creating links between worksheets can really save us time because when we update the source worksheet, Excel updates any linked worksheets for us. Obviously, links help cut down on typographical errors, too.

Creating Graphs

Excel shares the graphing program, Microsoft Graph, with the other members of Microsoft Office. If you're new to Graph, this section will serve as a good introduction to the features and flexibility of this graphing program.

With Excel, we can create graphs in three ways: on the current worksheet, as a separate sheet in the current workbook, or in another workbook. In this section, we show you how to quickly plot a graph on the current worksheet. The advantage of this method is that we can then print the graph and the underlying worksheet on the same page. Let's create a column graph based on the income and expenses data in the Annual sheet:

1. Select A5:E5 in the Annual sheet, hold down the Ctrl key, and select A7:E7.

Noncontiguous ranges

The ChartWizard button

2. Click the ChartWizard button, move the cross-hair pointer to the blank area below the income statement, hold down the mouse button, and drag to create a *marquee*—a box—about 10 rows high by 5 columns wide. (Don't worry about the precise size and location for now.) When you release the mouse button, the ChartWizard displays the first of five dialog boxes to lead you through the process of creating and customizing a graph:

3. Click Next, both to confirm that you want Graph to plot the range you selected and to move to the next dialog box:

4. Select 3-D Column as the graph type and then click Next to display this dialog box:

5. Accept the default 3-D column type (4) by clicking Next. Graph displays in the fourth dialog box how the selected range will look as a graph, with all labels and other information in place:

6. Accept the default settings and move to the fifth dialog box by clicking Next. (At any point, you can click the Back button to move back to a previous dialog box, so you can always select a different format if you change your mind.)

7. In the final dialog box, accept the default settings for a legend and click Finish. Graph plots this column graph:

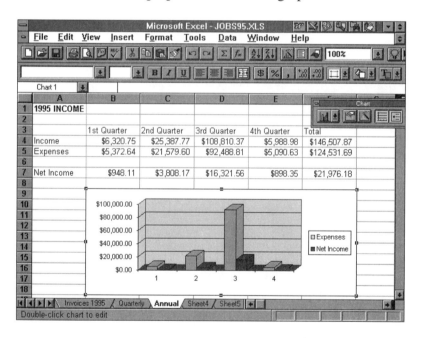

As you can see, four groups of columns, called *data markers*, represent the four quarters of data you selected. Within each group, one data marker represents the expenses category and the other represents the net income category. The data markers are identified in the legend by the labels from column A of the selected range: Expenses and Net Income.

Data markers

8. Click the Chart toolbar's Close box at the left end of its title bar to hide the toolbar and reduce screen clutter.

Sizing and Moving Graphs

As we mentioned, we don't have to worry about the precise size and location of the graph when we create it because we can always adjust it by dragging the small black squares, called *handles*, around the graph's frame. Try this:

Handles

1. Point to the handle in the middle of the left side of the frame and drag it toward the center to decrease the graph's width.

Changing height and width proportionally

2. Drag a corner handle diagonally inward to decrease both the height and the width proportionally.

3. Move the entire graph by pointing anywhere inside its frame and dragging in the direction in which you want to move.

4. When you've finished experimenting, restore the graph to its original size and location.

Updating Graphs

Graph has actively linked the graph to its underlying data, so if we change the data, Graph will redraw the graph to reflect the change. To demonstrate graph updating, let's now restore the original amount in cell E22 of the Invoices 1995 worksheet:

1. Click the Invoices 1995 tab and enter *1898.46* in cell E22.

2. Next click the Annual tab. The updated graph looks like this:

Adding values to an existing series

If you add values to a set of data in your worksheet and want to update a graph you created earlier to reflect the new values, you can select the values and simply drag the selection to the graph. When you release the mouse button, Graph adds the additional data points along the category axis.

Changing the Graph Type

No matter what type of graph you need—area, bar, pie, line, and so on—Graph has a format that will probably do the job. You can always come up with impressive visual support for a worksheet by carefully selecting from among Graph's many predefined graph types. Let's try changing the type of the graph currently on your screen so that you can see some of the possibilities:

1. Double-click anywhere within the graph to select it. If your graph fits in the worksheet window, Graph surrounds the graph with a shaded border and handles. If the graph's frame stretches beyond the edges of the worksheet window, Graph opens the graph in its own window. Either way, Graph changes the menus on the menu bar to accommodate the commands appropriate for working with graphs.

2. Choose Chart Type from the Format menu to display the dialog box shown here:

3. Select 2D in the Chart Dimension section and then select the Line option and click OK.

   Graph draws a graph in which the expenses and net income data are represented as two separate lines on the graph as shown on the next page.

The default graph format

Initially, Graph creates graphs in its default format—a two-dimensional column graph. To change the default format to the format of the active graph, choose Options from the Tools menu and click the Chart tab. In the Default Chart Format section, click Use The Current Chart, assign the graph format a name in the Add Custom AutoFormat dialog box, and click OK. The new name then appears in the Default Chart Format box. Click OK again. Any new graph you create will then be in this format. The new default format remains in effect until you change it.

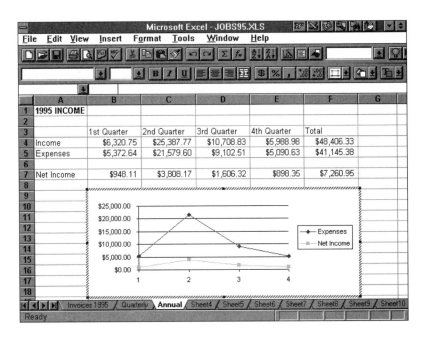

4. Choose Undo Chart Type from the Edit menu to restore the previous type.

5. Display the Chart Type dialog box and double-click the 3-D Pie option. Now the four quarters of expenses data are represented as colored wedges in a three-dimensional pie graph. You no longer see the net income data because a pie graph can display only one set of data.

X-axis and y-axis

Graph uses the terms *x-axis* and *y-axis* with some of its commands. For clarification, here are a couple of definitions: The x-axis shows the information categories—for example, expenses and net income; the y-axis shows the data points (plotted values).

6. Select other graph types from the Chart Type dialog box to get an idea of what's available. Then finish up with a simple two-dimensional column graph.

Using Graph AutoFormats

Often, selecting one of the options in the Chart Type dialog box will produce exactly the graph we need, but sometimes we might want something slightly different. Before spending time adjusting the format of a graph type, it's worth exploring Graph's *autoformats*. Follow these steps:

1. With the graph selected, choose AutoFormat from the Format menu to display this dialog box:

Because a column graph is active, Column is selected as the graph type in the Galleries list, and the default column autoformat, number 6, is highlighted in the Formats section.

2. Select 3-D Bar from the Galleries list to display the gallery of 3-D bar autoformats shown here:

Adding notes

To add explanatory notes to a graph, select the graph (but check that no other graph element is selected), click an insertion point in the formula bar, type the note, and press Enter. Graph displays a text box containing the note in the middle of the graph. You can use the handles around the text box to reposition it or resize it. To format the text box and the note it contains, choose Selected Object from the Format menu, and make your selections on the tabs of the Format Object dialog box.

3. Click format number 5 and then click OK. The result is shown below:

You might want to explore some of the other available graph autoformats. In particular, try creating a combination graph, which plots one type of graph on top of another as an "overlay" (see the adjacent tip).

Previewing and Printing Graphs

Previewing and printing graphs is much like previewing and printing worksheets. We can preview and print the worksheet data and graph together or just the graph. Follow these steps:

1. Click anywhere outside the graph to deselect it, click cell A1, and then click the Print Preview button. As you can see, one or two adjustments would greatly improve the look of this page.

2. Click the Close button to return to the Annual worksheet. Then adjust the position and size of the graph so that it is centered on columns A through F and separated from the worksheet entries by about five rows of blank cells (see page 120).

Combination graphs

To create a combination graph, select Combination from the Galleries list in the AutoFormat dialog box and then select one of the autoformats. You can plot your data as one graph type overlaid by another graph type—for example, a column graph overlaid by a line graph. If your data includes series that span widely divergent ranges of values, you can plot the data against two y-axes of different scales—for example, one series against a y-axis on the left of the graph ranging from 0 to 100 and another series on the right of the graph ranging from 100,000 to 1,000,000.

3. Click the Print Preview button again and then click the Setup button on the Print Preview toolbar.

4. Click the Margins tab, change the Top margin setting to *1.5*, and in the Center On Page section, select the Horizontally option.

5. Click the Header/Footer tab, click the arrow to the right of the Header option, and select (none) from the top of the drop-down list. Repeat this step for the Footer option.

6. Click the Sheet tab, click the Gridlines option to deselect it, and click OK. Here are the results:

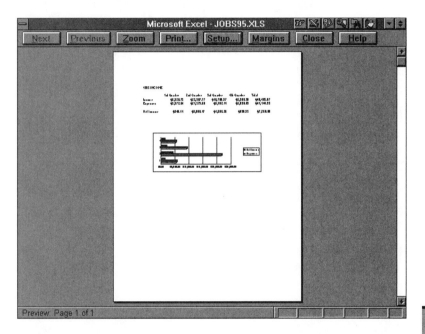

If you want, you can now click the Print button to create a paper copy of your graph.

Chapters 4 and 5 have given you a quick overview of Excel. To explore this program further, you might want to check out *A Quick Course in Excel 5 for Windows*, which discusses this powerful spreadsheet in more detail.

Printing graphs only

To print a graph without its underlying worksheet, double-click the graph to select it, and click the Print button on the Standard toolbar. (Or choose the Print command from the File menu, be sure the Selected Chart option is selected in the Print dialog box, and click OK.)

6
PowerPoint Basics

Include the subject, speaker, and company on the title slide

Use bulleted list slides to make your points succinctly

Add subordinate bullets for secondary items

Create two presentations and then merge them

Make a bigger impact by using just a few bulleted items

Change the look of a presentation by changing its template

PowerPoint is the presentation component of Microsoft Office, and it's packed with all sorts of tools to simplify the task of creating presentations. From good old reliable transparencies to electronic slide shows with "flying bullets," PowerPoint does it all.

In this chapter, we cover the basic steps for developing Power-Point presentations. We introduce you to the AutoContent Wizard and the Pick A Look Wizard, which help you decide on the text and design of a presentation. We also show you how to add a just the look you want to a presentation by changing its template.

Using the AutoContent Wizard

For our first presentation, we're going to let the AutoContent Wizard be our guide. The AutoContent Wizard asks a few questions to get the ball rolling and then allows us to select one of six sample presentations as a starting point. Follow these steps to start PowerPoint and use the AutoContent Wizard:

The Microsoft PowerPoint button

1. Click the Microsoft PowerPoint button on MOM's toolbar. The first time you start PowerPoint, you are invited to take a tour of the program. Click Cancel to close the window. You then see the Tip of the Day, which draws your attention to a particular feature, trick, or shortcut.

2. Deselect the Show Tips At Startup option and click OK. Power-Point then displays this dialog box:

As you can see, you can start a new presentation in one of four ways, or you can open an existing presentation.

3. Click the AutoContent Wizard option and then click OK to display the first of four AutoContent Wizard dialog boxes:

4. Read the information in the dialog box and then click Next to move to this dialog box:

The information you enter in this dialog box will become the first slide, called the *title slide*, of the presentation. In the middle and bottom edit boxes, PowerPoint may have entered the name and company name used when the program was installed. The sample to the left gives you an idea of what the title slide will look like.

The title slide

5. Type *Toward a Healthy Environment* in the top edit box, replace the name in the middle edit box with *Ted Lee*, and in the bottom edit box replace the company name with *Redmond Business Environmental Action Team*. Click Next to display the third dialog box shown on the next page.

Entering the title slide text

Presentation do's and don'ts

Using a program like PowerPoint won't ensure that your presentations will be successful. You have to use some common sense, too. Here are some tips for creating clear, concise presentations:

- Know as much as possible about your audience before you start creating your presentation and tailor its tone, words, and graphics appropriately.

- What points do you want your audience to remember after your presentation? Come up with an overall theme that you can reinforce throughout the presentation.

- Make each slide convey only one main idea that can be interpreted at a glance.

- Cut the verbage on each slide to the essentials. Never have more than six bulleted items on a slide. The more bulleted items you have, the fewer words you should use in each item.

- Make sure your capitalization and punctuation are consistent. On any one slide, don't mix complete sentences and partial sentences.

- Above all, don't expect your slides to carry the entire weight of the presentation. To hold the attention of your audience, you must be poised and confident, and you must express your ideas clearly and persuasively.

The titles of the slides in the selected presentation are shown on the left. You can click each option in turn to see which one most closely resembles the presentation you want to create.

6. Click the Recommending A Strategy option and click Next to display the dialog box shown here:

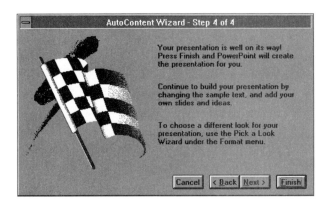

7. Read the information in the final AutoContent Wizard dialog box and click Finish. PowerPoint opens two new windows: the presentation window and the Cue Cards window.

8. The Cue Cards window gives tips for working in PowerPoint. You can explore the Cue Cards feature later by choosing Cue Cards from the Help menu, but for now, double-click the Control menu icon at the left end of the Cue Cards title bar to close this window. Then click the Maximize button at the right end of the presentation window's title bar to expand the window as shown at the top of the facing page:

Outlining toolbar

Standard toolbar

Formatting toolbar

Slide title

Bulleted items

Taking up most of the screen is the new presentation, which PowerPoint displays in outline view. The first topic is the title-slide information we entered in the second AutoContent Wizard dialog box. The remaining topics are PowerPoint's suggestions as to the items we might want to cover when recommending a strategy. Each topic supplied by PowerPoint is designated by a number and a small slide icon to indicate that the topic will appear as the title of a slide. Subtopics are indented and bulleted to indicate that they will appear as bulleted items on their respective slides.

Before we go any further, we should save the presentation:

1. Click the Save button on the toolbar to display the Save As dialog box.

2. Type *redbeat1* in the File Name edit box (PowerPoint will automatically add the extension PPT), and click OK.

3. If PowerPoint displays the Summary Info dialog box, replace *Recommending a Strategy* in the Title edit box with *Redmond BEAT, Part 1*, and press Tab.

First impressions

In a strong presentation, each slide must stand on its own as well as contribute to the overall message, so when you first start creating presentations, you will probably want to work in slide view to see how each slide looks. Once you have a few presentations under your belt, you might find it quicker to work in outline view and then switch to slide view to see the results. In either case, you can go back and make changes at any time, so don't worry about getting stuck with something less than perfect. In fact, it's often best to leave the fine-tuning until the end of the development process; too much fussing can bog down even a short project.

4. In the Subject edit box, type *Introduction* and press Tab.

5. In the Author edit box, type *Ted Lee* and click OK to close the dialog box.

Working in Slide View

Above the status bar in the bottom left corner of the presentation window is a row of buttons that we use to switch from one view of a presentation to another. As mentioned, we are currently in outline view; notice that the Outline View button (second from the left) is "pressed." In this view, we can see all the topics and bulleted lists of the presentation in outline form. We use outline view mainly for reordering the topics and bulleted text of our presentations. Follow these steps to switch to slide view, where we can concentrate on the content of this presentation one slide at a time:

Outline view

Slide view

The Slide View button

1. Click the Slide View button. Your screen now looks like this:

Drawing toolbar

Slide

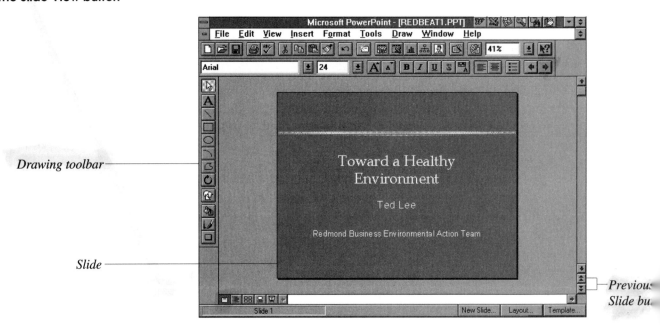

Previous Slide bu...

The Outlining toolbar has been replaced by the Drawing toolbar. Occupying the presentation window is a representation of the title slide of your presentation displayed with PowerPoint's default template, which controls the appearance of all the slides in the presentation (see page 146 for more information about PowerPoint's templates).

2. Click the Next Slide button at the bottom of the vertical scroll bar to move to the second slide, which looks like this:

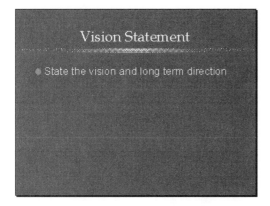

Editing Text in Slide View

You can work with text in both outline view and slide view. To edit the existing slides in slide view, follow these steps:

1. On Slide 2, select the text to the right of the bullet and type the following:

By the year 2000, all Redmond companies will have evaluated their business practices and implemented any changes necessary to promote a healthy environment

2. Save your changes.

Slide 2 looks pretty good, so let's move on:

1. Click the Next Slide button to display Slide 3.

2. Delete *and Objective* from the title and type *s* to turn *Goal* into *Goals*.

3. Click anywhere in the slide's bulleted list to activate the "object area" of the slide.

4. Click the bullet in front of *State the desired goal* to select the first bulleted item and type *Encourage win-win solutions*.

5. Repeat step 4 to replace the second bulleted item with *Stop waste*.

Moving among slides

In addition to the Previous Slide and Next Slide buttons, you can use the PageUp and PageDown keys and the scroll bar that appears on the right side of the presentation window in slide view to move from one slide to another. Simply point to the scroll box in the scroll bar, hold down the left mouse button, and drag the box up or down. As you drag, Power-Point displays the number of the slide that will appear when you release the mouse button at that point.

6. Repeat step 4 again to replace the third bulleted item with *Reduce the nation's garbage bill.*

Adding bulleted items

7. Press Enter. PowerPoint moves the insertion point to a new line, preceded by a bullet.

8. Type *Increase business awareness.* Here are the results:

Adding Subordinate Points

Sometimes you will need to add subordinate points below a main bullet in order to get your point across. Follow these steps:

1. Click the Next Slide button to move to Slide 4, click the title to activate the "title area" of the slide, select *Today's Situation,* and type *About Redmond BEAT.*

2. Change *Summary of the current situation* to *Publishes On the BEAT newsletter* and press Enter to create a new bullet.

3. Type *Supports local recycling efforts* and press Enter to create a new bullet.

4. Type *Chapter of USA BEAT* and press Enter.

The Demote button

5. Now click the Demote button on the Formatting toolbar. PowerPoint replaces the bullet with a chevron (») and indents the line to show that this point is subordinate to the preceding bullet.

6. Type *National office, Washington DC,* press Enter to create a new subordinate point, type *Chartered in 1989,* and then press Enter.

7. To stop adding subordinate points and create a new main bulleted item, click the Promote button. PowerPoint replaces the chevron with a bullet and moves the line back out to the margin.

The Promote button

8. Type *Maintains resource center* as the fourth bullet.

9. Finally, delete the *Use brief bullets* item by selecting the text and pressing the Backspace key twice to delete first the text and then the bullet. Slide 4 now looks like this:

Deleting bulleted items

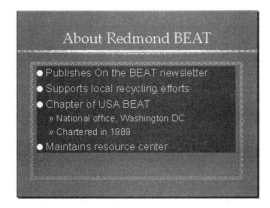

Deleting Slides in Slide View

Because we'll create the next four slides using the Pick A Look Wizard, we need to dispose of Slides 5, 6, and 7, which were provided by the AutoContent Wizard. Follow these steps to delete Slide 5 (we'll take care of Slides 6 and 7 in a moment):

1. Click the Next Slide button to move to Slide 5, which bears the title *How Did We Get Here?*

2. Choose the Delete Slide command from the Edit menu.

3. Now press the PageUp and PageDown keys to be sure the slide has truly been deleted.

Working in Outline View

We can edit slide text in outline view, but this view really shines when it's time to organize a presentation. Organizing is often a trial-and-error process. We start by evaluating the major topics, add and delete a few subtopics, and then move items around and

The fewer bulleted items the better

The default slide template allows you to enter eight single-line bulleted items on a slide, but eight is really too many. As we said in the tip on page 130, you will stand a better chance of getting your point across to your audience if you limit the number of bulleted items to no more than six single lines. The more bullets you have on a slide, the harder it is for your audience to focus on any one of the points you are trying to make. If you have many bulleted items, try to find ways of breaking them up into logical groups and use a different slide for each group.

change their levels. This task is easiest to accomplish in outline view because the Outlining toolbar puts the tools needed for organizing a presentation close at hand. Try this:

The Outline View button

1. Click the Outline View button in the bottom left corner of the presentation window to see the presentation you developed in slide view as a series of topics and subtopics.

2. Scroll the outline until you can see all the bulleted items under the *About Redmond BEAT* topic and click the bullet to the left of *Maintains resource center*.

The Move Up button

3. Click the Move Up button on the Outlining toolbar until the selected item sits above *Supports local recycling efforts*.

The Move Down button

4. Now click the chevron to the left of *National Office, Washington DC* to select the item, and click the Move Down button. The two subordinate points effectively switch places.

Selecting a bulleted group

5. Click the bullet to the left of *Chapter of USA BEAT*. PowerPoint selects not only the text adjacent to the bullet but also its two subordinate points.

6. Click the Move Up button three times. PowerPoint moves the main bullet and its subordinate points to the top of the *About Redmond BEAT* list, which now looks like this:

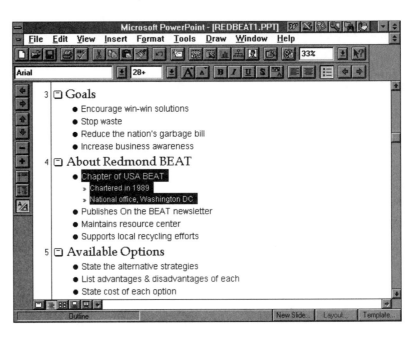

Here's another way to rearrange bulleted items:

1. Under the *Goals* topic, click the bullet to the left of *Increase business awareness*.

Reorganizing by dragging

2. Point to the selected text, hold down the left mouse button, drag the shadow insertion point until it sits to the left of the *E* in *Encourage* and release the mouse button. PowerPoint moves the selection to its new location at the top of the bulleted list.

   As you scroll through the outline of the presentation, you might notice a slide or two that would work better in a different location. However, if the outline is too long to fit on the screen all at one time, it is sometimes hard to decide on a precise order for the slides. The solution is to collapse the outline so that only the main topics are visible, like this:

The Show Titles button

1. Click the Show Titles button on the Outlining toolbar and then scroll to the beginning of the presentation. PowerPoint has hidden all the bulleted items and put a gray line under each topic to indicate the presence of hidden information, as shown here:

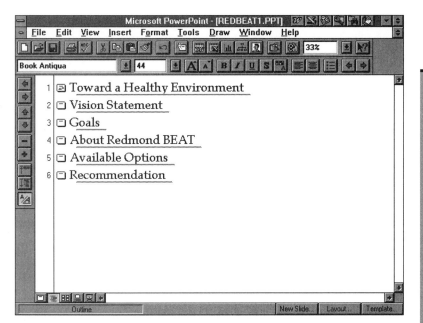

Selecting parts of a slide

You can use many of the standard Windows text-selection techniques when editing text in both outline and slide views. For example, you can double-click a word to select it. In both views, you can click a bullet to select the bulleted item and its subordinate bullets. In outline view, you can click the slide icon to the left of a topic to select the topic and all of its bulleted items. In slide view, you can select an entire text object, such as a bulleted list, by clicking the object and then either choosing Select All from the Edit menu or pressing Ctrl+A.

2. Click to the left of the number of Slide 4 to select the slide and its hidden text, and then click the Move Up button until *About Redmond BEAT* is the second topic in the outline.

The Expand Selection button

3. Verify that the hidden text moved with the topic by clicking the Expand Selection button. Here's the result:

The Collapse Selection button

4. Click the Collapse Selection button to once again hide the bulleted items.

The Show All button

5. Click the Show All button to display the entire outline in its new order.

Deleting Slides in Outline View

Deleting a slide in outline view is a simple editing process. Follow these steps to delete Slides 5 and 6:

1. Click to the left of the number 5 and press Delete.

2. Repeat step 1 to delete the new Slide 5 (old Slide 6), and then press Backspace to delete the slide image.

3. Save and close the presentation.

Using the Pick A Look Wizard

While the AutoContent Wizard provides both the design and content for a presentation, the Pick A Look Wizard helps us select a design for a presentation but leaves the content entirely up to us. Let's use the Pick A Look Wizard to create a second presentation:

The last slide

If you click the Next Slide button after you reach the end of a presentation provided by the Auto-Content Wizard, PowerPoint beeps and displays the message *This is the last slide in the active presentation* in the status bar. To add another slide to the presentation, use the New Slide button at the bottom of the presentation window or the New Slide command on the Insert menu. For more information about adding slides, see page 142.

1. Click the New button on the Standard toolbar and in the New Presentation dialog box, click Pick A Look Wizard and then click OK. PowerPoint presents you with the first of nine dialog boxes. Take a moment to examine the dialog box's contents and then click the Next button.

2. In the wizard's second dialog box, check that **On-Screen Presentation** is selected as your output option and click Next.

Setting up for an electronic
slide show

3. In the third dialog box, which offers several design template options, click the More button to display this dialog box:

4. Double-click the TEMPLATE directory in the Directories list.

   PowerPoint's built-in templates are stored in the three subdirectories: BWOVRHD, CLROVRHD, and SLDSHOW. As their names suggest, these directories contain templates that can be used to create three specific types of output: black and white overheads, color overheads, and slides for a slide show.

5. Double-click the SLDSHOW directory to display the names of the templates for slide shows. Click any template name in the File Name list to display a sample of the template that appears in the bottom right corner of the Presentation Template dialog box. Press the Up and Down Arrow keys to scroll through the templates, noticing their different looks.

6. When you're ready, select the FORESTS.PPT template and click the Apply button. PowerPoint returns you to the wizard's third dialog box, with a sample of the FORESTS.PPT template displayed on the left.

The Template option

You can bypass the Pick A Look Wizard's dialog boxes and go straight to the Presentation Template dialog box by selecting the Template option in the initial PowerPoint dialog box. After you select a template, PowerPoint displays the New Slide dialog box so that you can select a layout for your first slide. You can then create your presentation by adding text, charts, graphics, additional slides, and so on in the usual way.

7. Click the Next button to display the fourth dialog box, which allows you to generate additional types of output, such as speaker's notes, audience handouts, and outline pages.

8. To create slides only, deselect the three options below the Full-Page Slides option and click Next to display this dialog box:

9. Select the Name option, enter *Redmond BEAT* in the accompanying edit box, and click Next.

10. In the final dialog box, click Finish to display the template in slide view, like this:

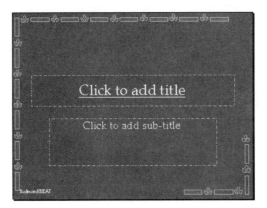

11. Save the presentation with the name *redbeat2*. In the Summary Info dialog box, type *Redmond BEAT, Part 2* in the Title edit box, type *Introduction* in the Subject edit box, type *Ted Lee* in the Author edit box, and then click OK.

Adding Slide Text

Suppose we want to begin this presentation with some thought-provoking information. Let's start by changing the layout of the current slide to one that will accommodate a bulleted list. Here are the steps:

1. Click the Layout button at the bottom of the presentation window to display this dialog box:

Changing the slide layout

PowerPoint provides 20 predefined slide layouts, called *Auto-Layouts*, plus one "clean slate" that you can use to design a slide layout of your own. You can scroll the other AutoLayouts into view by using the scroll bar to the right.

AutoLayouts

2. Select the Bulleted List AutoLayout (the second AutoLayout in the first row), and click Apply.

Slide 1 is now ready and awaiting our input. Follow these steps:

1. Click the title area and type *The Cost of Waste in the U.S.* as the slide's title.

2. Click the object area and type *Today: $10 billion* as the first bulleted item.

3. Press Enter to start another bulleted item and then type *By the year 2000: $100 billion.* (By the way, the source for these statistics is *The Recycler's Handbook*, published by Earth Works Press in Berkeley, California.)

Adding Slides

Unlike the AutoContent Wizard, which provides a series of slides for you to use, the Pick A Look Wizard provides only the initial slide. To add three more slides to the presentation, follow these steps:

1. Click the New Slide button at the bottom of the presentation window to display the New Slide dialog box, which is almost identical to the Slide Layout dialog box (see page 141).

2. With the Bulleted List AutoLayout selected, click OK to add a second slide to your presentation.

3. Click the title area of Slide 2 and type *How Much Waste?*

4. Type *Residences: 850 million tons* as the first bulleted item and *Industry: 6.5 billion tons* as the second bulleted item, pressing Enter to start the second bulleted item.

5. Repeat steps 1 and 2 above to add a new bulleted list slide and then type *Where Do I Start?* as the title.

6. Click the object area of Slide 3 and type the following two bulleted items:

   • *Join Redmond BEAT*

   • *Attend meetings at 8:00 AM on the last Tuesday of every month*

7. Add a fourth bulleted list slide, and type *What Can I Do?* as the title. Then type the following bulleted items:

   • *Start a recycling program*

   • *Educate employees*

   • *Buy post-consumer products*

   • *Call Ted Lee at 555-6789 for more suggestions*

Repositioning text objects

You can use the mouse to reposition text objects on a slide. For instance, if you want to shift the title up a bit, click the title area to select it, point to the frame surrounding the area, hold down the left mouse button, and then drag the frame upward. You can use this same technique to reposition the object area on a slide. In addition, you can resize text objects by dragging the handles that appear when an object is selected.

Moving Text Between Slides

If you take a look at Slide 4, you'll notice that the fourth bulleted item might be better suited for Slide 3. We can easily move the text to Slide 3 using a little cutting and pasting, like this:

1. With the object area of Slide 4 activated, click the fourth bullet to select the bulleted text.

2. Click the Cut button to remove the text from the slide and store it temporarily on the Clipboard.

3. Click the Previous Slide button to move to Slide 3, click an insertion point at the end of the second bulleted item, press Enter to create a new bullet, and then click the Paste button to paste the bulleted text onto Slide 3, which looks like this:

The Previous Slide button

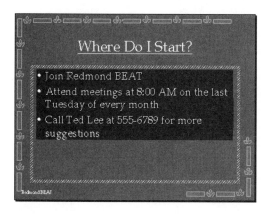

4. Now move to Slide 4, click an insertion point just after the fourth bullet, and press the Backspace key to remove the extra bullet.

Merging Presentations in Slide Sorter View

In slide sorter view, we can see the slides of a presentation laid out visually. Sketches, called *thumbnails*, display the slides in enough detail that we can get a pretty good idea of how they

Slide sorter view

look. We can then make adjustments to the presentation by adding or deleting slides or changing their order. Slide sorter view is also a good place to merge presentations because we can see and control the merging process. Follow these steps to get ready to merge REDBEAT2.PPT with REDBEAT1.PPT:

The Slide Sorter View button

1. Click the Slide Sorter View button in the bottom left corner of the presentation window. Your screen looks like this one:

2. Now choose REDBEAT1.PPT from the bottom of the File menu and click the Slide Sorter View button. (If REDBEAT1.PPT is not one of the four most recently opened files, use the Open command to open the file.)

3. Choose the **Arrange All** command from the Window menu to place both presentations side by side.

4. To decrease the size of the slide thumbnails so that you can to see all the slides of both presentations at the same time, click the arrow to the right of the Zoom Control box on the Standard toolbar of the active window, and select 25% from the drop-down list. Then do the same thing in the other window. Your screen looks like this:

Now we can combine the two presentations:

1. Select all of the slides in the active REDBEAT2.PPT presentation by choosing Select All from the Edit menu.

2. Point to any one of the selected slides, hold down the left mouse button, and drag the dotted vertical marker to just after Slide 4 in the REDBEAT1.PPT presentation.

Merging presentations with drag-and-drop

3. Release the mouse button to drop the REDBEAT2.PPT slides into place. PowerPoint renumbers the merged slides and overwrites the design template of REDBEAT2.PPT with that of REDBEAT1.PPT.

4. Close the REDBEAT2.PPT window, clicking No when Power-Point asks whether you want to save your changes.

Reordering Slides in Slide Sorter View

Now that we've merged the two presentations, suppose we decide that Slides 7 and 8 need to be transposed. Here are the steps for reordering slides in slide sorter view:

1. Maximize the REDBEAT1.PPT window and select 50% from the Zoom Control drop-down list to increase the size of the slide thumbnails.

Increasing the thumbnail size

2. Click any blank area and then click Slide 8 to select it, hold down the left mouse button, and drag the vertical marker to the left of Slide 7. When you release the mouse button, Slides 7 and 8 switch places, like this:

The Show Formatting button

The Show Formatting button is the last button at the right end of the Slide Sorter toolbar. When you click this button, PowerPoint removes the formatting, as well as the design template, from the current slides, leaving only the slide titles. Removing the formatting and design template can be a real time-saver because Power-Point does not have to "redraw" the slides every time you make a change to your presentation in slide sorter view. To restore the formatting and design template, click the Show Formatting button again.

Applying Templates

The appearance of a presentation is controlled by the template we select. As a result, we can change the entire look and feel of a presentation by simply switching to another template. As you saw in the Presentation Template dialog box shown on page 139, PowerPoint offers a wide variety of design templates to choose from. Follow the steps below to see how easy it is to reapply the FORESTS.PPT template:

1. With REDBEAT1.PPT displayed on your screen in slide sorter view, click the Template button at the bottom of the window to open the Presentation Template dialog box.

2. Double-click the SLDSHOW directory, if necessary, and scroll down to the FORESTS.PPT file.

3. Double-click FORESTS.PPT to apply it to your presentation. The slides now look like this:

4. Save and close the presentation.

Now that you've learned how to create presentations with both the AutoContent Wizard and the Pick A Look Wizard, you're ready to start exploring ways of enhancing presentations. In the next chapter, we show you how to add graphs and organization charts to your presentations so that you can wow your audiences with visual information.

7

More About PowerPoint

Create an organization chart to illustrate a company hierarchy

Add as many boxes and levels as you need

Adjust the size and position of the object area

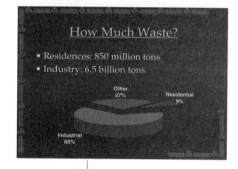

Create and format a graph to visually present numeric data

Select the chart type that best suits the data you are plotting

Words and numbers are nice, but visual representations of your words and numbers can really make an audience sit up and take notice. There's nothing like a line graph to show the fluctuations in sales over the past six months or an organization chart to show the current management structure of a corporation. In this chapter, we cover the ins and outs of adding graphs and charts to your presentations, and we also show you how to run an electronic slide show so that you can see a presentation in action on your computer.

Adding Graphs

PowerPoint shares the Microsoft Graph graphing program with other Office members. In this section, we show you how to add a couple of graphs to the REDBEAT1.PPT presentation. We'll use a graph AutoLayout to add the first graph and the Insert Graph button to add the second graph. We'll also give you a few pointers about working with graph objects and manipulating a graph on a slide.

Using a Graph AutoLayout

Let's add a graph to the REDBEAT1.PPT presentation we created in Chapter 6 by changing the layout of Slide 5:

1. With PowerPoint loaded, open REDBEAT1.PPT in slide view and move to Slide 5.

2. Click the Layout button at the bottom of the presentation window and when the Slide Layout dialog box appears, select the Text & Graph AutoLayout (the second AutoLayout in the second row), and click Apply. Slide 5 now looks like this one:

New graph slides

If you want to create a brand new graph slide instead of adding a graph to an existing slide, you can simply click the New Slide button at the bottom of the presentation window, select one of the graph AutoLayouts in the New Slide dialog box, and then click OK.

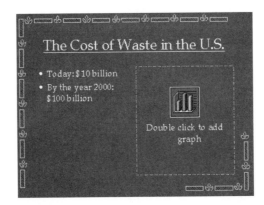

3. Double-click the graph placeholder to start Microsoft Graph. Your screen looks something like this:

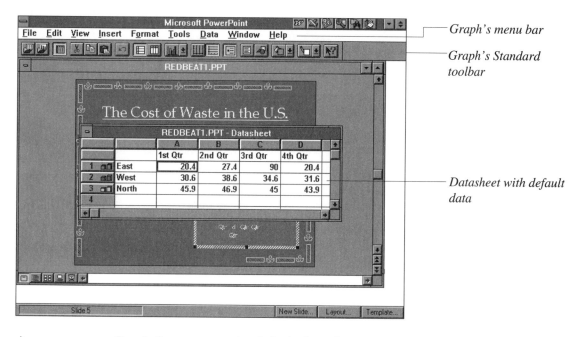

Graph's menu bar

Graph's Standard toolbar

Datasheet with default data

As you can see, Graph first presents its default *datasheet*, which resembles an Excel worksheet. Gridlines divide the datasheet into cells. In the leftmost column and topmost row are column and row headings, or *labels*. We can edit and format these labels like any other text in PowerPoint. Above the column labels and to the right of the row labels are column letter and row number buttons. Depending on whether the data is organized by column or by row (see the adjacent tip), markers appear on the column letter or row number buttons to indicate the current graph type.

Let's replace the "dummy" data in the datasheet with our own information. (By the way, this data is fictitious and is used for demonstration purposes only.) Start with the labels:

1. Select the first cell in column A (the cell that contains *1st Qtr*) by clicking it with the mouse. (Be careful not to click outside the datasheet or graph. If you do, Graph automatically returns you to PowerPoint. You must then double-click the graph on the current slide to start Graph again.)

The datasheet

By row or by column

You can arrange the data series in your datasheet by row or by column. Graph assumes that the series are arranged by row; but if you have arranged the series by column, you can ensure that Graph will plot your data correctly by clicking the By Column button on Graph's Standard toolbar. If you want to return to the by-row arrangement, click the By Row button. Graph places miniature markers on the row number buttons of the datasheet if the data series are arranged by row and on the column letter buttons if the data series are arranged by column.

2. Type *1995*, press Tab to move to the first cell in column B, and type *2000*.

3. Select the first cell in row 1 (the cell that contains *East*), type *U.S.*, press Enter to move to the first cell in row 2, type *Europe*, press Enter again, and type *Japan*.

To speed up the entry of the remaining data in the datasheet, try this technique:

Quick data entry

1. Point to the second cell in column A and drag to the third cell in column B to select the block of cells.

2. Now type *10*, press Enter, type *6*, press Enter, type *7.5*, and press Enter again. In the next column, type the data shown below, pressing Enter after each number:

100
57
75

3. Choose Save from Graph's File menu to save your work.

Now you can plot the graph. You don't want to plot the "dummy" data in columns C and D, so first exclude it by doing this:

Excluding data

1. Click column C's letter button, hold down the Shift key, click column D's letter button, and release the Shift key.

2. With both columns selected, choose Exclude Row/Col from Graph's Data menu.

The View Datasheet button

3. Click the View Datasheet button to remove the datasheet and display the new graph, which looks like this:

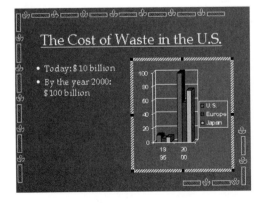

Obviously, we'll have to make some cosmetic adjustments, such as fixing some of the labels and repositioning the graph on the slide.

Changing the Graph Type

With Graph, we can easily switch from one graph type to another if we're not satisfied with the way our data is displayed. For clarity, change the type of the graph on Slide 5 by following these steps:

1. Choose the Chart Type command from Graph's Format menu to display this dialog box, where the current type, 3-D column, is highlighted:

2. Select the 2-D option in the Chart Dimension section and then double-click the Column option. Graph inserts a 2-D column graph on Slide 5, like this:

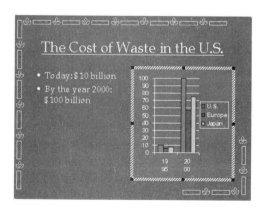

Adjusting column width

To increase or decrease the width of a column in a datasheet, select the column (click the corresponding column letter button), choose Column Width from Graph's Format menu, and enter a number in the Column Width dialog box. Click the Best Fit button in the Column Width dialog box to automatically adjust the column width to fit the longest entry in the column. You can also use the mouse to change the column width. Simply point to the border that separates adjacent column letter buttons, and when the pointer changes to a vertical bar with two arrows, hold down the left mouse button and drag to the left or right. If you double-click the border between two column letter buttons, the width of the column on the left is automatically adjusted to fit the longest entry. You can select multiple columns and use any of the methods described above to change the width of all the selected columns simultaneously.

Adding a Title

We can add a title to the graph as a whole, to the category (x) axis, to the value (y) axis, or to all three. Try adding a title to the column graph in REDBEAT1.PPT now:

1. Choose the Titles command from Graph's Insert menu to display this dialog box:

2. Select the Chart Title option and click OK. Graph adds a title placeholder to the chart area.

3. Double-click the placeholder text to select it, type *In Billions of Dollars*, and then click away from the title but inside the graph frame.

Formatting a graph title →
4. Now point to the title and click once to select it. (You'll know the title is selected when graph surrounds it with a frame and handles.)

5. Choose Selected Chart Title from Graph's Format menu to display the dialog box shown here:

6. Click the Alignment tab, select the Top option in the Vertical section, and click OK. The title shifts upward to give you a little more room.

Adding an axis title

To add a title to a graph's axis, choose Titles from Graph's Insert menu, select the appropriate option in the Titles dialog box, and click OK. Then, when the axis title placeholder appears, type the text of the title. If you want to rotate the title, first select it and choose Selected Axis Title from Graph's Format menu. Next, click the Alignment tab of the Format Axis Title dialog box and select one of the options in the Orientation section.

Positioning and Sizing a Legend

By default, Graph has added a legend to the column graph in REDBEAT1.PPT. (If a graph does not have a legend, we can add one by clicking the Legend button on Graph's Standard toolbar.) Follow these steps to reposition and resize the legend:

The Legend button

1. Click the legend once to select it. (Be sure the entire legend is selected, not one of the legend entries or keys.)

2. Point to the border surrounding the legend (not a handle) and then drag upward until the legend is positioned just below the graph's title.

Repositioning a legend

3. Click anywhere inside the graph's frame to deselect the legend. (Be careful not to click *outside* the graph's frame, or you'll wind up back in PowerPoint.) The graph now looks like this:

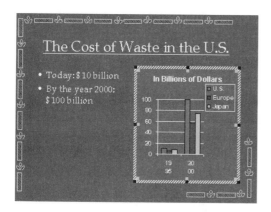

Adjusting Tick-Mark Labels

The two-dimensional column graph in REDBEAT1.PPT has two axes: the *value* or vertical y axis and the *category* or horizontal x axis. (Some three-dimensional graph types have a third axis, called the *series* axis.) We can format the axes in a variety of ways, but here we'll focus on the small marks used to group values or categories along their axes, which are called *tick marks*, and the labels accompanying the tick marks are called *tick-mark labels*. As you can see, the two tick-mark labels along the category (x) axis of the column graph need to be realigned so that they are legible. To make this adjustment, follow the steps on the next page.

Changing label position

By default, Graph places tick-mark labels next to their respective axes. You can change the position of the labels by selecting one of the Tick-Mark Labels options on the Patterns tab of the Format Axes dialog box. Selecting the Low or High option places labels next to the minimum or maximum values of the other axis, respectively. Selecting the None option removes the labels altogether.

1. Click the category (x) axis and choose Selected Axis from Graph's Format menu to display the Format Axis dialog box.

2. On the Alignment tab, select the second vertical option in the Orientation section, and click OK. Here are the results:

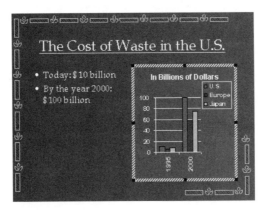

Adding a Border

So that the graph, title, and legend hang together as a unit on the slide, we can surround the chart area with a border. Follow these steps to add a heavy yellow border to the column graph:

1. Click a blank area of the graph to select the chart area and choose Selected Chart Area from Graph's Format menu. Graph displays the Format Chart Area dialog box.

2. On the Patterns tab, click the arrow to the right of the Color edit box in the Border section to display the Color palette.

3. Select the yellow box in the first row of the palette.

4. Next click the arrow to the right of the Weight edit box, select the last option (heavy), and click OK.

5. Click anywhere outside the chart area to return to PowerPoint.

6. Finally, click anywhere outside Slide 5 to deselect the graph. The results are shown at the top of the facing page.

The Color and Pattern buttons

To quickly add color or a pattern to any graph object, select the object, click the Color or Pattern button on Graph's Standard toolbar, and select the desired color or pattern.

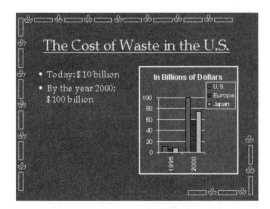

Moving and Sizing Graphs

We don't have to open Graph to move and resize the chart area of a graph. We can accomplish these tasks in PowerPoint, like this:

1. Choose Ruler from the View menu to turn on PowerPoint's rulers. (The rulers will serve as guides when you move and resize the graph.)

2. Click the column graph in REDBEAT1.PPT once to select it.

3. Point anywhere inside the graph's border, hold down the mouse button, and when the dashed positioning box appears, drag to the left about 1/2 inch, using the horizontal ruler as a guide.

   As you can see, the bulleted text is crowding the graph a bit. To rewrap the text, follow these steps:

1. Activate the object area by clicking anywhere in the bulleted text. Then click the frame surrounding the object area to select the area.

   Rewrapping text by resizing the object area

2. Drag the right center handle to the left about 1 inch. As the size of the object area decreases, the bulleted text rewraps.

   Now finish resizing the graph by increasing its width:

1. Click the graph to select it, point to the left center handle, and when the pointer changes to a double-headed arrow, drag to the left 1/2 inch.

2. Choose Ruler from the View menu to turn off the rulers and then deselect the graph to see the results shown here:

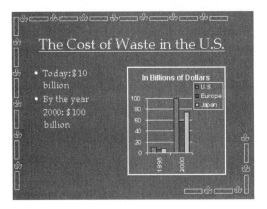

Using the Insert Graph Button

The second method of adding a graph to an existing slide involves using the Insert Graph button on PowerPoint's Standard toolbar. Follow these steps to add a 3-D pie graph to Slide 6:

The Insert Graph button

1. With REDBEAT1.PPT open in slide view, move to Slide 6 and click the Insert Graph button on the Standard toolbar.

2. When the default datasheet appears, complete it as shown here (we used the mouse to widen column A so that the entire Residential heading is visible):

		A	B	C	D	
		Residential	Industrial	Other	4th Qtr	
1	Waste	0.85	6.5	2.65	20.4	
2	West	30.6	38.6	34.6	31.6	
3	North	45.9	46.9	45	43.9	
4						

REDBEAT1.PPT - Datasheet

3. Use the Exclude Row/Col command on Graph's Data menu to exclude rows 2 and 3 and column D from the graph.

Now, instead of using the Chart Type dialog box to change the graph type, try the following:

The Chart Type button

1. Click the arrow to the right of the Chart Type button on the toolbar to display this palette of options:

2. Click the 3-D pie icon (the fifth icon in the right column).

3. Now click the View Datasheet button. The 3-D pie graph looks like this:

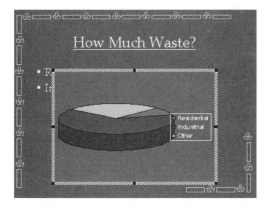

4. Point to the top center handle of the graph's chart area and then drag down until the graph no longer obscures the bulleted text of the slide.

Adding Data Labels

In addition to the labels along the axes in graphs, we can add labels to the data markers themselves. These labels can even show the value or percent of each marker and can include the legend key. Follow these steps to add data labels to the pie graph:

1. Select the legend and press the Delete key. (The data labels you're going to add will make the legend redundant.)

Rotating a pie graph

To rotate a pie graph, choose the 3-D Pie Group command from the bottom of Graph's Format menu or the Format 3-D Pie Group command from the bottom of the shortcut menu. When the Format 3-D Pie Group dialog box appears, click the Options tab, enter the number of degrees you want to rotate the pie in the Angle Of First Slice edit box, and click OK. Your pie graph is displayed at the bottom of the Options tab so that you can see the effects of your changes.

2. Choose Data Labels from Graph's Insert menu to display this dialog box:

3. Select the Show Label And Percent option and click OK.

The plot area of the pie graph has been reduced to accommodate the labels, which now appear next to their respective data markers. Increase the size of the plot area and then reposition the data labels by following these steps:

Resizing the plot area

1. Click the plot area—the area occupied by the graph itself—to select it, point to the bottom right handle, and drag downward. Then drag the other corner handles until the graph has approximately doubled in size.

Repositioning data labels

2. Now click the Industrial label to select it, point to its frame, and drag the label until it is touching its marker.

3. Repeat step 2, dragging the other two labels to their respective markers, like this:

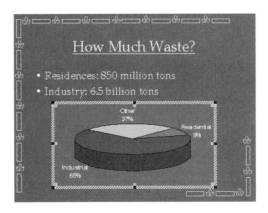

Separating Slices

In pie graphs, we can separate the individual markers, or slices, by simply dragging them with the mouse. As you'll see if you follow these steps, separating the slices helps to distinguish them:

1. Click the Residential marker to select it. (Selecting individual markers is often a tricky process. You know when a single marker is selected because it's the only one surrounded by handles.)

2. Point to the marker and drag away from the center of the pie.

3. Repeat step 2 for the Industrial data marker. Here's what the graph looks like after you return to PowerPoint:

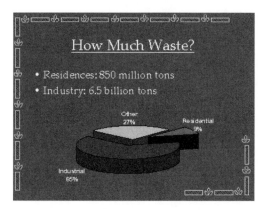

Adding Organization Charts

If you flip back to page 149, you'll see an organization chart on the second slide of the REDBEAT1.PPT presentation. As its name suggests, an organization chart, henceforth known as an *org chart*, shows hierarchy, such as the executive branch of a corporation. With a little imagination, the basic org chart elements can also be used to develop flow charts that illustrate processes.

In this section, we'll create an org chart to depict the structure of USA BEAT, the environmental group from which Redmond BEAT got its start. Follow these steps:

1. With REDBEAT1.PPT open, display Slide 2 in slide view.

Adding an org chart to an existing slide

You can add an org chart to an existing slide in one of two ways. The easiest way is to move to the slide in slide view, and then click the Insert Org Chart button on the Standard toolbar. When the org chart window opens, you can complete the org chart as usual. A second, more involved, technique is to use the Object command on the Insert menu. First move to the slide in slide view, and choose Object from the Insert menu. When the Insert Object dialog box appears, be sure the Create New option is selected, and then double-click the Microsoft Organization Chart 1.0 option in the Object Type list. As before, the org chart window opens so that you can complete the org chart.

2. Click the New Slide button at the bottom of the presentation window and when the New Slide dialog box appears, double-click the Org Chart AutoLayout (the third AutoLayout in the second row) to add an org chart slide to the presentation.

3. Double-click the org chart placeholder in the slide's object area to display a window like the one shown here:

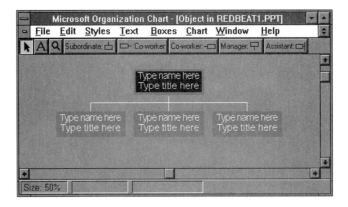

Microsoft Organization Chart

Like Microsoft Graph, Microsoft Organization Chart is a program within a program. As you can see, the org chart window has its own menu bar, toolbar, and status bar.

4. Click the Maximize button at the right end of the org chart window's title bar to maximize the window.

Adding a title

5. Select the text of the chart title placeholder with the mouse (you may have to scroll the window to see this placeholder), and type *Business Environmental Action Team*.

Before we go any further, let's change the interior color of the org chart's boxes so that we can more easily see the contents. (This step is not always necessary; however, this org chart reflects the color scheme we selected in Chapter 6, and some adjustments are needed here.) Follow these steps:

Changing the color of the boxes

1. Click any of the boxes, hold down the Shift key, and click the remaining boxes to select them.

2. Choose Box Color from Org Chart's Boxes menu and then select black from the drop-down list of colors.

With this detail out of the way, we're ready to fill in the org chart's boxes:

1. Click the topmost box to select it, type *Northwest BEAT* as the name, and press Enter.

Filling in the boxes

2. Type *Olympia, WA* as the title, and press Enter.

3. For the first comment, type *Regional Office*, and then click the leftmost subordinate box to select it.

4. Type *Washington BEAT*, press Enter, and type *Seattle, WA*.

5. Click the second subordinate box, type *Oregon BEAT*, press Enter, type *Portland, OR*, and click outside the box. Here are the results:

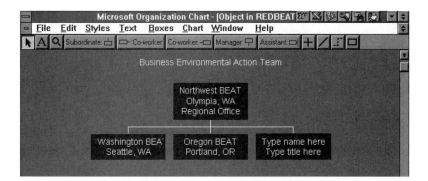

6. Choose Update REDBEAT1.PPT from Org Chart's File menu to update the REDBEAT1.PPT presentation.

Updating a presentation

To actually save the org chart as part of the presentation, we must return to PowerPoint and save it there (see page 167). Again, we won't tell you to update from this point on, but you should remember to do so often.

Saving an org chart

Adding and Removing Boxes

We aren't limited to the four boxes the Org Chart program has provided. We can add and remove boxes with just a few mouse clicks. Try this:

1. To add a box to the top of the org chart, click the topmost box to select it, click the Manager button on the Org Chart toolbar, move the mouse pointer (which is now shaped like a manager box) to the selected box, and click once.

The Manager button

2. In the new manager box, type *USA BEAT*, press Enter, and type *Washington, DC*.

Assistant: ⊏||

The Assistant button

3. Next, select the Northwest BEAT box, click the Assistant button on the Org Chart toolbar, and then click the Northwest BEAT box to add an assistant box to the org chart.

4. In the assistant box, type *Redmond BEAT*.

Subordinate: ⊐‖

The Subordinate button

5. Add two subordinate boxes to Washington BEAT by clicking the Washington BEAT box to select it, clicking the Subordinate button on the Org Chart toolbar twice (note that the status bar displays *Create: 2*), moving the mouse pointer (which is now shaped like a subordinate box) to the Washington BEAT box, and clicking once.

6. In the new subordinate boxes, type *Vancouver BEAT* and *Spokane BEAT*, respectively.

7. Repeat step 5 to add two subordinate boxes to Oregon BEAT.

8. In the new subordinate boxes, type *Salem BEAT* and *Medford BEAT*, respectively.

Deleting boxes

9. Remove the "empty" box next to Oregon BEAT by selecting it and pressing Delete. The org chart now looks like this one:

Org chart size

When you create an org chart for a PowerPoint presentation, remember to maintain a reasonable size for the org chart. If your org chart is too small, viewers may not be able to read the contents of the org chart boxes. In addition, if your org chart contains several boxes, you might consider breaking the org chart up and placing it on separate slides so that viewers aren't overwhelmed with information.

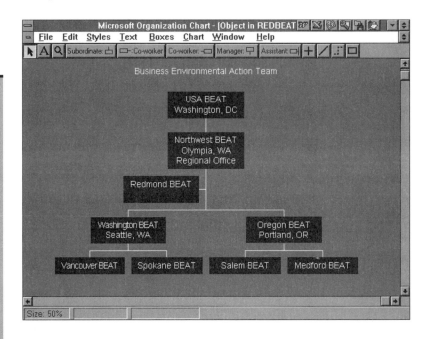

Rearranging Boxes

If we're not happy with the arrangement of boxes in an org chart, we can use the mouse to rearrange them in a variety of ways. Try the following:

1. Point to the Oregon BEAT box, hold down the left mouse button, and drag the box's frame over the Washington BEAT box. As you move the box, notice the shape of the mouse pointer. A left-pointing arrow indicates that the box will appear to the left of the existing box; a right-pointing arrow indicates that the box will appear to the right of the existing box; and a subordinate box indicates that the box will appear below the existing box.

2. When the pointer changes to a left-pointing arrow, release the mouse button. The Washington BEAT and Oregon BEAT boxes switch places. (Notice that the subordinate boxes below Oregon BEAT and Washington BEAT have moved as well.)

3. Now point to the Redmond BEAT box, hold down the left mouse button, and drag the box's frame over the bottom half of the Washington BEAT box. When the pointer changes to a subordinate box, release the mouse button.

4. Deselect the Redmond BEAT box and using the techniques you've just learned, move the box to the left of the Vancouver BEAT box. After all that reshuffling, here are the results:

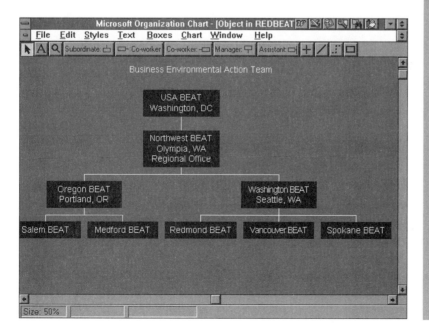

Magnifying an org chart

You can use the commands on Org Chart's Chart menu to adjust the magnification of an org chart. The following list describes each command:

- Size To Window displays the entire org chart in the org chart window.
- 50% Of Actual displays the org chart at 50% of Actual Size.
- Actual Size displays the org chart at approximately 50% larger than its printed size.
- 200% Of Actual displays the org chart at 200% of Actual Size.

You can also use the Enlarge button on the Org Chart toolbar (the button with the magnifying glass icon) to zoom in on areas of the org chart. After you click the Enlarge button, the Reduce button (the button with the org chart icon) appears in its place so that you can zoom out. (The Reduce button has the same effect as the Size To Window command.)

Switching Styles

In Org Chart jargon, a *group* refers to the subordinates under a manager, and a *branch* refers to a manager plus all its subordinates. By default, groups are placed side by side in boxes, as in the sample org chart; however, the Org Chart program offers several style alternatives for both groups and branches. Experiment with some of the other org chart styles by following these steps:

1. Select the Redmond BEAT box and press Ctrl+G to select its group, which consists of all three Washington BEAT subordinate boxes.

2. From Org Chart's Styles menu, choose the second style in the first row. The org chart looks like this:

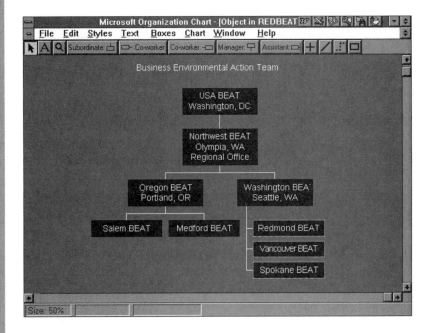

3. Next select the Salem BEAT box and press Ctrl+G.

4. If two or more members of an organization share the same manager as well as the same responsibilities, those members can be designated as comanagers. To designate the selected boxes as comanagers, choose the Co-manager style from Org Chart's Styles menu by clicking its icon.

Now condense the org chart by changing the style of its main branch:

Groups and branches ────────────────▶

Formatting org charts

You can format the text, boxes, and connecting lines in an org chart by using the commands on Org Chart's Text and Boxes menus. All of these commands are self-explanatory, so we don't need to go into a lot of detail here. Suffice it to say that most of the commands on the Text and Boxes menus are followed by an arrowhead, which indicates that a drop-down list of options will be displayed when you choose that command. You can then simply click the option you want. The only exceptions are the Font and Alignment commands on the Text menu. If you choose the Font command, a Font dialog box similar to other Font dialog boxes appears. You can change the font, style, and size of the org chart text by selecting options in this dialog box. To change the alignment of the org chart text, simply choose Left, Right, or Center from the Text menu. Keep in mind that before you can use any of these commands, you must select the text, boxes, and/or lines you want to format. The easiest way to make your selection is to use the Select or Select Levels command on Org Chart's Edit menu. For example, to select all the connecting lines in an org chart, choose Select and then Connecting Lines from the Edit menu.

1. Select the USA BEAT box and press Ctrl+B to select its branch—
   the entire org chart.

Selecting a branch

2. From Org Chart's Styles menu, choose the third style in the first
   row. Here are the results:

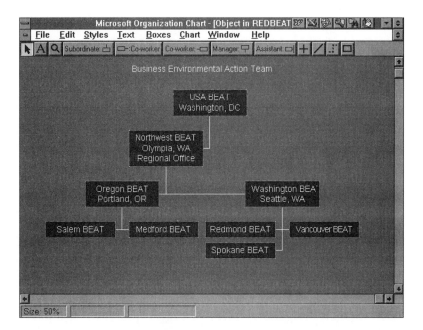

3. If the capital *T* in *Washington BEAT* is cut off, with the entire
   org chart still selected, choose Left from Org Chart's Text menu
   to realign the text.

Returning to PowerPoint

After the org chart is complete, quitting Org Chart and returning
to PowerPoint automatically adds the org chart to the current
slide. Once the org chart is in place, we can use the mouse to
reposition or resize it. (We can return to the Org Chart program
at any time by double-clicking the org chart on the slide.) Follow
these steps to return to PowerPoint:

1. Choose Update REDBEAT1.PPT from Org Chart's File menu.
   (If you don't choose this command first, you will be prompted
   to update the org chart before proceeding.)

Quitting Microsoft Organization
Chart

2. Choose the Exit And Return To REDBEAT1.PPT command
   from Org Chart's File menu.

Back in PowerPoint, several adjustments are needed. First, we need to remove the slide's title placeholder because the org chart comes equipped with a title. Second, we need to resize the org chart to fill the current slide. Follow these steps:

1. Click the title area of the slide, press F2 until the title placeholder is surrounded by handles, and then press Delete to remove the placeholder.

2. Click the object area once to select the org chart, point to the top center handle, and when the pointer changes to a double-headed arrow, drag upward a couple of inches.

3. Use the side handles to widen the org chart about 1/2 inch on both sides. Here are the final results:

4. Save the presentation.

If we want to save the org chart as a separate file, we can use the Save Copy As command on Org Chart's File menu.

Running an Electronic Slide Show

To output a PowerPoint presentation on paper or on acetate (to create overhead transparencies), we can use the Print button. We can also send a PowerPoint file to a graphics service bureau if we want to output the presentation as a set of 35mm slides (see the adjacent tip). However, to really impress an audience and simultaneously take advantage of the latest technology, we can turn a presentation into an electronic slide show, complete with special effects. In this section, you'll learn how to view an electronic slide show on your own computer and how to add transitions and builds to the presentation. Let's get going:

1. With REDBEAT1.PPT open on your screen, move to Slide 1 and click the Slide Show button at the bottom of the presentation window to display the title slide of the presentation in slide show view, like the one shown here:

The Slide Show button

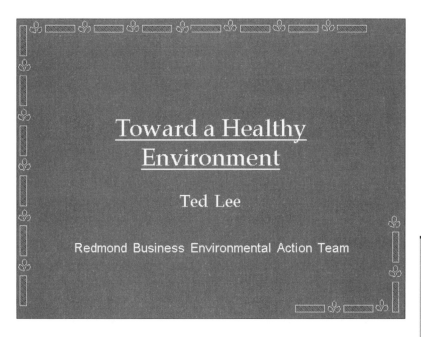

2. Click the left mouse button to move to the next slide, and continue clicking the button until you reach the slide with the title *Where Do I Start?*.

3. Click the right mouse button to return to Slide 8, which bears the title *What Can I Do?*.

Rather than clicking the right mouse button to return to Slide 1, try this alternative:

1. Type *1* and press Enter.

2. Press the Esc key to return to slide view.

Displaying selected slides

If you only want to show specific slides from a presentation during a slide show, choose the Slide Show command from the View menu to display the Slide Show dialog box. Then, in the Slides section of the dialog box, enter the numbers of the slides you want to show in the From and To edit boxes, and click Show. The first of the selected slides instantly appears in slide show view. As always, you can use the mouse buttons and the PageDown and PageUp keys to move through the other slides in the presentation and then press Esc when you're finished.

Adding Transitions and Builds

To spruce up an electronic slide show, we can add *transitions* and *builds*. Transitions are special effects that help move the audience smoothly from slide to slide. Builds, on the other hand, help keep the audience focused on a particular point by constructing slides one bulleted item at a time. Let's add transitions to all the slides except the title slide, and then add builds to Slides 2, 5, 8, and 10:

Specifying a transition →

1. Click the Slide Sorter View button to switch to slide sorter view, and then select Slides 2 through 9 by holding down the Shift key as you click each slide.

2. Click the arrow to the right of the Transition Effects box on the Slide Sorter toolbar, select Blinds Vertical from the drop-down list, and watch Slide 2 carefully as PowerPoint demonstrates the effect of the transition you have selected. PowerPoint also puts a transition icon below the slides with transitions.

Specifying a build →

3. Deselect Slides 3, 6, 7, and 9. (Hold down the Shift key as you click the slides to deselect them.)

4. Click the arrow to the right of the Build Effects box on the Slide Sorter toolbar and select Fly From Right from the drop-down list. PowerPoint puts a build icon below the slides with builds.

Let's check out the effects we've added by running the slide show again:

Testing transitions and builds →

1. Select Slide 1 (to be sure the slide show starts at the beginning of the presentation) and click the Slide Show button.

2. Click the left mouse button to move to Slide 2 and then click it again to bring each bulleted item into view.

3. Move through all the slides so that you can see the transitions and builds in action.

4. Do a little experimenting with the other transitions and builds that PowerPoint offers and then run through the slide show again.

5. When you're ready to leave slide show view, press Esc.

Now that you have an understanding of how PowerPoint works, you can forge ahead on your own to create professional presentations. If you want to learn how to produce even more sophisticated presentations, check out *A Quick Course in PowerPoint 4 for Windows*, which expands on the information given here.

Access Basics

Specify an input mask to minimize invalid entries

Set the maximum size for entries, depending on their type

Employees   4/30/95

Emp#	SS#	First Name	Last Name	Address	City	Zip	Phone#	First Day
002	796-29-4473	Carol	Talbot	1109 Emerson Way	Lakewood	98403	334-7625	27-Aug-79
019	228-12-9111	Ron	Westerman	1419 Ivy Drive	Pinedale	98412	335-1326	08-Sep-85
027	854-72-2249	Fred	Anderson	943 Spruce Circle	Lakewood	98403	832-8779	14-Feb-89
033	583-02-1253	Lance	Bright	148 Center St, #B211	Pinedale	98412	334-6683	23-Jun-91
034	477-11-6309	Richard	Talbot	1109 Emerson Way	Lakewood	98403	334-7625	04-Jun-93
035	722-52-2624	Linda	Gardner	8841 Market Street	Lakewood	98403	334-6754	02-May-94
037	455-82-9921	Jefrey	Davis	1171 Simpson Heigh	Lakewood	98403	334-9297	12-Jun-94
038	241-21-4972	Jonathan	Bray	5941 Hilltop Road	Lakewood	98403	334-0180	17-Jun-94

Substitute captions for cryptic field names

Specify a date format so that entries are displayed consistently

Specify how many digits a field entry must contain

Use a wizard to efficiently create database tables and then customize them

Set a default entry that Access will enter unless you enter something else

Y ou are probably excited but nervous about learning to use a powerful database like Microsoft Access. And you're probably hoping that, like the other Office applications, Access will be simple to use and yet offer you the tools you need to handle complex data. Well, relax. By the end of this chapter, you will be familiar enough with Access to be able to start creating databases to meet most of your needs.

Database tables

Before we load Access, let's discuss the concept of a database. The most basic component of an Access database is a *table*—a collection of information arranged in *records* (rows) and *fields* (columns). A database can consist of several tables of related data. For example, a client database might assign clients a number and list their names and addresses in one table and then list their numbers and credit references in another. Still another table might summarize account transactions for the last three years by client number. All the tables contain information about the clients, but each table has different information that is related by the client number. All the information could be kept in just one table, but if only a few clients have active accounts, the part of the table devoted to account transactions would have only a few entries. So it's more efficient to break the database into separate but related tables.

Other database components

Tables are the basic building blocks of a database. In addition to tables, a database can include queries, forms, reports, and other components, all of which allow us to view and manipulate database information in a variety of ways. As you follow along with our examples, you will create a database for Tip Top Roofing that includes several of these components.

Setting Up a Database

Without any more preamble, let's fire up Access and set up the example database, which is called Roofs. Access will then store all the tables, queries, forms, and reports we create as we work our way through Chapters 8 and 9 in the Roofs database file. Follow these steps:

1. Click the Microsoft Access button on the MOM toolbar. The first time you start Access, you see this window, which suggests six ways of learning and getting started with Access:

The Microsoft Access button

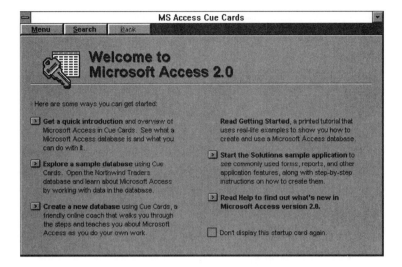

2. You don't want to see this screen everytime you start Access, so click the Don't Display This Startup Card Again option in the bottom right corner, and then double-click the Control menu icon at the left end of the MS Access Cue Cards title bar. You then see the empty Access window with a title bar, a menu bar, a toolbar, and a status bar.

3. Click the New Database button on the toolbar to display this dialog box:

The New Database button

4. Type *roofs* in the File Name edit box and press Enter. Access displays the database window shown on the next page.

Cue Cards

You can display Cue Cards at any point while you are working with Access to get help with basic tasks and procedures. Just click the Cue Cards button (second from the right on the toolbar) to display a window with a list of available topics, and click the topic you want. To close the window, double-click its Control menu icon.

Down the left side of the window are buttons for each type of database component. Clicking one of these buttons displays in the box to the right a list of the existing components for that type. Because this is a new database, the Table option is selected, and the box is empty.

Creating a Table

We can now create the first table in the database, which will be used to store information about Tip Top Roofing's employees. Follow these steps:

Table wizards

1. In the database window, click New. Access opens this dialog box, in which you specify whether you want the Access table wizards to help you set up the new table or whether you prefer to do the setup work yourself:

2. Click Table Wizards to display the first of a series of dialog boxes that lead you through the steps of creating your table's field structure:

3. In the Sample Tables list, click Employees. The Sample Fields list changes to reflect the kind of information usually stored in an employee database, with EmployeeID selected.

4. Click the > button to add the EmployeeID field name to the Fields In My New Table list.

5. Add the SocialSecurityNumber, FirstName, LastName, Address, City, PostalCode (Zip code), HomePhone, and DateHired field names to the Fields In My New Table list by clicking each name and then clicking the > button. Then click the Next button to display the next wizard dialog box:

6. The name Access suggests for this database—Employees—is pretty logical, so don't change the entry in the edit box. However, you don't want Access to set the *primary key*, which is a field that distinguishes one record from another. When you enter field values in the table, no two entries in this field can be the same.

Allowing Access to create the primary key

If you allow Access to create the primary key, Access inserts a Counter field as the first field of the table, designates that field as the primary key, and automatically enters a consecutive number as that field's value for each record.

In keyed tables, if you try to enter the same field value in two records, Access displays an error message and won't let you move to a new record until you change one of the duplicates. Click the Set The Primary Key Myself option and then click Next. The next wizard dialog box appears:

7. Because you want to set up the primary key yourself, you must now tell Access which field you want to use and what type of data that field will contain. You do want to use the default Employee ID as the primary key, but instead of allowing Access to enter consecutive numbers as the primary key, you want to enter the numbers yourself. Click the second option button and then click Next. The final wizard dialog box appears:

8. Click the Finish button to indicate that you want to enter data directly in the table. Access displays this table window:

Entering and Deleting Records

Each record in the Employees table will contain information about one employee. In Access, you can enter and edit records either directly in the table in datasheet view, which displays as many records as will fit on the screen in column/row format, or in a form in form view, which displays one record at a time. We'll look at both methods in this section.

Datasheet view vs. form view

Entering Records in a Table

Because you told the table wizard that you wanted to enter data directly in the table, Access has already switched the new table to datasheet view. An insertion point sits blinking in the Employee ID field, ready for you to enter the first item of information, and an arrowhead in the record selector at the left end of the row indicates that the record is ready to receive data. Let's enter the first item now:

1. Type *2* as the first employee number. The arrowhead in the record selector changes to a pencil, indicating that the data in the record has been changed but not yet saved. (Access has added a second record with an asterisk in its record selector, indicating that the record is empty.) Press Enter to move the insertion point to the next field.

2. Enter the field values in the first record shown on the next page, pressing Enter to move from field to field.

> **Fields and records**
>
> The basic structure of a database is a combination of fields and records. Each field contains bits of similar information—for example, all the phone numbers in the phone book. Each record contains all the bits of information about a particular item such as a person, product, or event—for example, the name, address, and phone number for one person in the phone book.

Field	Record 1
Social Security Number	796294473 (Access inserts the hyphens)
First Name	Carol
Last Name	Talbot
Address	1109 Emerson Way
City	Lakewood
Postal Code	98403 (Access adds a hyphen)

Don't worry that the data in the Address field doesn't fit within its column; we'll fix that in a minute.

3. Click the Home Phone field, click an insertion point to the right of the area code's open parenthesis, and press the Right Arrow key three times. Then type *3347625* and press Enter.

4. In the Date Hired field, type *08/27/79*, and press Enter.

5. Enter records 2 through 5 as shown below, remembering to use the Right Arrow key to skip over the area code in the Home Phone field:

Field	Record 2	Record 3	Record 4	Record 5
Employee ID	19	27	29	33
Social Security Number	228129111	854722249	934218635	583021253
First Name	Ron	Fred	James	Lance
Last Name	Westerman	Anderson	Murray	Bright
Address	1419 Ivy Drive	943 Spruce Circle	7921 Port Avenue	148 Center St, #B211
City	Pinedale	Lakewood	Lakewood	Pinedale
Postal Code	98412	98403	98403	98412
Home Phone	3351326	8328779	8345934	3346683
Date Hired	09/08/85	02/14/89	03/22/91	06/23/91

The Employees table now looks like this:

Fast navigation

When entering and editing data, using the keyboard to move around a window is often faster than using a mouse. You can easily navigate using the Arrow, Tab, Home, End, Page Up, and Page Down keys.

Employee ID	Social Security	First Name	Last Name	Address	Ci
2	796-29-4473	Carol	Talbot	1109 Emerson Way	Lakewoo
19	228-12-9111	Ron	Westerman	1419 Ivy Drive	Pinedale
27	854-72-2249	Fred	Anderson	943 Spruce Circle	Lakewoo
29	934-21-8635	James	Murray	7921 Port Avenue	Lakewoo
33	583-02-1253	Lance	Bright	148 Center St, #B2	Pinedale

Now let's widen the Address field. Follow these steps:

1. Move the pointer to the gridline between the Address and City field names.

Widening fields

2. When the pointer changes to a double-headed arrow, hold down the left mouse button, and drag to the right. When you think all the entries in the field will be visible, release the mouse button.

Here's another way to change the widths of fields:

1. Scroll the table to the right until the last four fields are visible. Move the pointer to the City field name, and when the pointer changes to a downward-pointing arrow, click to select that field in all records. Then move the pointer to the Date Hired field name, hold down the Shift key, and click to add the Postal Code, Home Phone, and Date Hired fields to the selection.

Selecting multiple fields

2. Choose Column Width from the Format menu to display this dialog box:

3. Type *15* and press Enter to change the widths of all four fields at the same time.

You might want to take some time to practice resizing the Employees table's fields; for example, try shrinking the fields enough to see all of them at one time.

Entering Records in a Form

Instead of entering information in a table, we can enter it in a *form*. To display a form for the Employees table and see how easy it is to enter records in a form, follow these steps:

1. Click the AutoForm button on the toolbar to display the form shown on the next page. (We've enlarged the window a bit.)

The AutoForm button

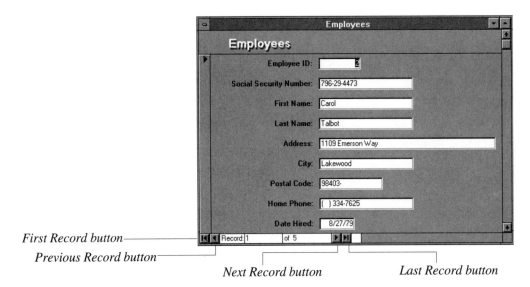

First Record button
Previous Record button

Next Record button   *Last Record button*

2. Click the Next Record button at the bottom of the window to display the information for Ron Westerman.

3. Click the Last Record button to move to the last record in the table and then click the Next Record button to display a blank record. Or simply click the New Record button on the toolbar.

The New Record button

4. Enter the record for the sixth employee. After typing the last field value, press Enter to display a new blank record, enter the record for the seventh employee, and press Enter.

Field	Record 6	Record 7
Employee ID	34	35
Social Security Number	477116309	722522624
First Name	Richard	Linda
Last Name	Talbot	Gardner
Address	1109 Emerson Way	8841 Market Street
City	Lakewood	Lakewood
Postal Code	98403	98403
Home Phone	3347625	3346754
Date Hired	06/04/93	05/02/94

The Employees table is complete for now, and we can view the records in either form view or datasheet view. Here's how to switch back and forth:

1. Click the Datasheet View button on the toolbar. Instead of the form, you now see the table.

The Datasheet View button

2. Click the Form View button on the toolbar to switch back to the form.

The Form View button

3. Close the form by double-clicking the form window's Control menu icon, and click No when Access asks whether you want to save the form. (The records themselves are already saved because Access automatically saves each record when you move to another one.)

The Employees table is now visible, but the records we entered via the form are not displayed. We need to update the table by following this step:

1. Click the Show All Records button on the toolbar. Access updates the table to show the last two records.

The Show All Records button

Deleting Records

To delete a record, we simply select the record and choose the Delete command. Follow these steps to delete a record from the Employees table:

1. Select James Murray's record by clicking its record selector and choose Delete from the Edit menu or press the Delete key. Access displays this dialog box:

2. Click OK. Access deletes the record and updates the table.

Be careful when deleting records. If you make a mistake and delete the wrong record, you can't restore the record by clicking an Undo button or choosing Undo from the Edit menu once you've confirmed the deletion.

Delete with caution

Changing a Table's Structure

When we used the table wizard to set up thc Employccs table, Access made a number of decisions about the table's basic design. But those decisions are not cast in stone. Let's examine the existing table structure and see how to change it:

The Design View button

1. Click the Design View button on the toolbar. Access displays the structure of the table in this window:

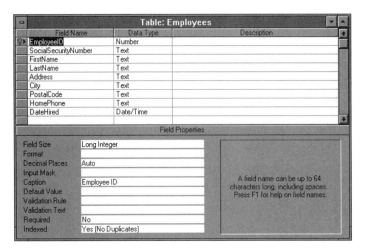

As you can see, the window is divided into two sections. The top half lists the table's field names (with no spaces) and their data type. (Specifying the data type determines what kind of information you can put in the field and how Access can work with the information.) The bottom half lists the properties assigned to the field selected in the top half.

2. Press Enter to move to the Data Type column for the EmployeeID field and click the arrow that appears to display a list of the available data types.

3. Click Number to close the Data Type list without changing its setting and press Enter to move to the Description column.

4. Type *Unique 3-character number identifies each employee.* When the table is displayed and this field is selected, this description will appear in the status bar.

After we define a field for a table, we can refine our field definitions in the Field Properties section. You will use some of

---

Access data types

Help with data types

Access is much more rigid about its data types than Excel is about its number formats. For example, specifying a Currency number format for a cell in Excel does not prevent you from entering text in that cell. In Access, you cannot enter text in a field that has been assigned the Number data type, For more information, choose Search from the Help menu, enter *data type*, double-click *data types: field*, and then double-click Choosing A Field Data Type.

these properties frequently, others rarely. Here, we'll explore the more common properties.

Setting the Field Size

We can set a field size for the text and number data types. For text fields, the size indicates the maximum number of characters we can enter in the field. We can specify up to 255 characters, which can include letters, numbers, and other characters such as &, %, and ?. If we try to enter, paste, or import a field value that is longer than the specified size, Access truncates the data. Follow these steps to set the size of the text fields of the Employees table:

1. Click anywhere in the SocialSecurityNumber field in the top table grid to display the default properties for that field in the Field Properties section.

2. Double-click *30* in the Field Size edit box to select it, and type *11* to indicate that the field can have up to eleven characters.

3. Repeat steps 1 and 2 to assign the following field sizes:

Field	Size	Field	Size
FirstName	10	City	12
LastName	12	PostalCode	10
Address	25	HomePhone	20

For number fields, the size is determined by the complexity of the data type format selected. The options are: ◄───── **Number field size**

Format	Description
Byte	Whole numbers between 0 and 255
Integer	Whole numbers between –32,767 and 32,768
Long Integer	Whole numbers between –2,147,483,647 and 2,147,483,648
Single	Single-precision floating-point numbers between –3.402823E38 and 3.402823E38
Double	Double-precision floating-point numbers between –1.79769313486232E308 and 1.79769313486232E308

Follow the steps on the next page to set the size of the table's number field.

1. Click anywhere in the EmployeeID field and then click the Field Size edit box in the Field Properties section.

2. Click the arrow to see a list of available sizes. You don't think the company will ever employ more than 255 employees, so select Byte.

Setting the Format

We use the Format property to specify how the characters entered in a field are to be displayed on the screen. The type of formatting we can perform varies depending on the data type. For example, we can select one of several predefined formats for date/time fields, like this:

Predefined formats → 1. Click anywhere in the DateHired field and then click the Format edit box in the Field Properties section.

2. Click the arrow to see a list of predefined formats, and select Medium Date. The dates in the table will now be displayed in dd-mmm-yy format.

In addition to selecting predefined formats, for some data types we can specify custom formats. Follow these steps to tell Access to always display three digits in the EmployeeID field:

Custom formats → 1. Click anywhere in the EmployeeID field and then click the Format edit box.

2. Type *000* to tell Access to enter three digits, using zeros unless you enter something else. Now if you enter an EmployeeID of *36*, Access will display the entry as *036*.

Specifying an Input Mask

Formats aren't the only way to control the display of data. We can also specify an *input mask*, or character pattern, that not only determines how our data looks on the screen but also what kind of data can be entered in a particular field. Because we used a table wizard to set up the Employees table, Access has already specified input masks for some fields. Let's take a look at a few of these input masks and make any necessary changes:

1. Click anywhere in the SocialSecurityNumber field. The entry in the Input Mask edit box is *000\-00\-0000*. The zeros are place-

holders for digits that you must enter, and the backslashes indicate that the hyphens are literal characters that Access will insert for you.

2. Click the PostalCode field in the table grid. The entry in the Input Mask edit box is *00000\-9999*. Again, the zeros are placeholders for digits you must enter. The nines are placeholders for an optional four-digit Zip code extension. Access enters the hyphen whether or not you enter this extension.

3. Click an insertion point after the last 9 and press the Backspace key six times to delete all but the five zeros. Now Access will accept only five digits in this field. We can no longer enter a 4-digit extension.

Now let's adjust an input mask with some help from Access:

1. Click the HomePhone field in the table grid. The entry in the Input Mask edit box is *!\(999") "000\-0000*.

2. Click the Input Mask edit box and then click the Build button—the button with three dots to the right of the edit box. Click Yes when Access tells you it must save the table before proceeding, and when another message box warns you that the changes you have made to the field sizes of the table might result in a loss of data (see the adjacent tip), click OK to proceed. Access then displays this Input Mask Wizard dialog box:

The Input Mask Wizard

Data integrity

Always stop and think before changing the field sizes and input masks for your data. Such changes can result in data losses that will seriously affect the usability of some fields. For example, if you had entered area codes in the HomePhone field, changing the input mask might have resulted in the last three digits of the employees' phone numbers being chopped off.

3. Click Next to accept the default Phone Number option and display the dialog box shown on the next page.

The 9s in the parentheses indicate that a three-digit area code is optional, whereas the seven-digit phone number is required.

4. All the employees live in the same area code, so you want to enter only the seven-digit phone number without having to use the Right Arrow key to skip the area code. In the Input Mask edit box, click to the left of the first 0, and then press the Backspace key to delete *!(999)* and the extra space.

5. Click the arrow to the right of the placeholder edit box and select the underscore from the drop-down list.

Trying out a mask

6. Now click at the left end of the Try It edit box and type your phone number. Then backspace over the last four digits and try typing *abcd*. Access won't accept letters in the entry because the zeros in the input mask require the entry of digits.

7. Press Esc to clear the Try It entry, and click the Next button to display this dialog box:

8. Click Finish to accept the default setting in the last wizard dialog box and return to the table window.

In case you want to experiment further, here's a list of some common characters used in the Input Mask edit box, together with what they mean to Access:

Input mask characters

Character	Action
L	Require a letter.
?	Allow any letter; if no letter is entered, leave blank.
&	Allow any character.
0	Require a digit; if no digit is entered, insert 0.
#	Allow any digit; if no digit is entered, leave blank.
<	Convert all following characters to lowercase.
>	Convert all following characters to uppercase.
\	Insert the following character as entered.

You can remove an input mask at any time. For example, let's remove the input mask from the DateHired field:

1. Click anywhere in the DateHired field to display its properties.

2. Select the entry in the Input Mask edit box and press Delete.

Assigning a Caption

The Caption property enables us to substitute text for the field name when we display the table. The caption may simply repeat the field name with spaces added for readability, or it may display something different. Let's change a few of the captions specified by the table wizard when we created the table:

1. Click anywhere in the EmployeeID field to display its properties in the Field Properties section.

2. Click an insertion point to the right of the *p* in *Employee* in the Caption edit box, hold down the Shift key, and press the End key to highlight all but *Emp*. Then type #.

3. Repeat steps 1 and 2 to change the following captions:

Social Security Number to *SS#*
Postal Code to *Zip*
Home Phone to *Phone#*
Date Hired to *First Day*

When we display the table, the new captions will be displayed as field names above each column of information.

Setting a Default Value

The Default Value property lets us specify a field value that Access is to enter in the table automatically. Because Tip Top Roofing is small and most of the employees live in the same city, we can use this property for both the City and PostalCode fields to speed up data entry. Follow these steps:

1. Click anywhere in the City field to display that field's properties in the Field Properties section.

2. In the Default Value edit box, click to display an insertion point and then type *Lakewood* as the default city name.

3. Repeat steps 1 and 2 for the PostalCode field, specifying *98403* as the default value.

Now every record we enter in the new database table will have Lakewood as its City field value and 98403 as its PostalCode field value, unless we replace them with something else.

Requiring Entries

If we leave the table's field structure as it is, it would be possible to create incomplete employee records. To ensure that key information is always entered, we can specify that a field must have an entry. Try this:

1. Click the EmployeeID field, click the Required edit box, click the arrow, and then click Yes.

2. Repeat step 1 for all the other fields.

Other Properties

When we made the EmployeeID field the primary key for the table, Access changed that field's Indexed property to Yes (No Duplicates), meaning that the field is indexed and no duplicate values will be allowed. Only text, number, currency, and date/time fields can be indexed. When a field is indexed, Access can process queries, searches, and sorts based on the field more

The Indexed property

quickly. (If a few values will be repeated often in a field, as is the case with the City and PostalCode fields, then indexing the field will not save much processing time.) Data entry and editing may be slower with indexed fields because Access must maintain the index as well as the table.

We set the Validation Rule property for a field when we want Access to allow only specific field values to be entered in the field. The kind of rule we can set up varies with the field's data type. We can specify that a text field should contain one of a set of values—for example, the City field should contain only Pinedale or Lakewood. We can specify that a date field should contain only the current date or a date that falls within a certain range. With number fields, we can specify that Access should accept only a specific value, or we can use the greater than (>) and less than (<) signs to specify that field values must fall within a range. We can also specify that the values in a field must match the values in the same field in another table. When we set a validation rule for a field, we can use the Validation Text property to display a message when an unacceptable value is entered.

The Validation Rule property

The Validation Text property

We will rarely need to use the Allow Zero Length property (available for text fields). When this property is set to Yes, we can enter "" in a field to indicate that the field doesn't apply for this record. For example, we could enter "" to indicate that an employee doesn't have a phone, whereas simply skipping the field indicates that we don't know the phone number.

The Allow Zero Length property

Testing the Changes

Now let's return to the table to see the effects of our changes:

1. Click the Datasheet View button on the toolbar. Access tells you it must save the table before it can switch views.

2. Click OK. When Access asks whether you want to test the data in the table against the new properties, click Yes. Access then displays the table window.

3. Maximize the window and decrease the width of the fields so that you can see all the employee data at once, as shown on the next page.

The table reflects all the visual changes we made to its structure. The Emp# field displays three digits, and *Lakewood* and *98403* have been entered by default in the blank record at the bottom of the table. Let's add more employees to try everything out:

1. Click the Emp# field of the blank record at the bottom of the table, type *38*, and press Enter. Access enters *038* in the field.

2. Type the following information in the indicated fields (press Enter to skip over the City and Zip fields):

Field	Record 8	Record 9
Emp#		37
SS#	241214972	455829921
First Name	Jonathan	Jefrey
Last Name	Bray	Davis
Address	5941 Hilltop Road	1171 Simpson Heights
Phone#	3340180	3349297
First Day	06/17/94	06/12/94

3. Press Enter to complete and save Record 9.

As you enter the field values, notice the effect of the field properties specified as part of the table's structure.

Working with Records

In Chapter 9, we show you some fairly sophisticated ways of working with records. Here, we'll cover some simple methods of manipulating data so that we can locate the information we need.

Finding Specific Records

We often need to find either a particular record in a table or all the records that have something in common, so Access provides an easy way to locate records. As a demonstration, let's search the Employees table for a record that has Talbot in the Last Name field:

1. Select the Last Name field of any record by pointing to the left of the field value and, when the pointer changes to a hollow right-pointing arrow, clicking to highlight the field.

2. Click the Find button on the toolbar to display the Find dialog box shown here:

The Find button

3. Point to the Find dialog box's title bar, hold down the mouse button, and drag the dialog box downward so that you can see the table's records.

4. Type *Talbot* in the Find What edit box and click the Find First button. Access highlights the first field value that matches your specification.

Finding the first record

5. Suppose this is not the employee record you need to examine. Click the Find Next button in the dialog box to display the next record with Talbot in the Last Name field.

Finding subsequent records

6. Click the Close button to close the dialog box.

When dealing with a very large table, we can temporarily focus on a subset of the records in the table by using *filters*. Clicking the Edit Filter/Sort button on the toolbar displays a Filter window in which we can set up the criteria that define the subset. Clicking the Apply Filter/Sort button applies the filter to the records and displays the subset. Filters are closely related to *queries*, which you'll learn about in Chapter 9.

The Edit Filter/Sort button

The Apply Filter/Sort button

Moving Fields

By default, the fields are displayed in the order in which we entered them when we designed the table. We can change the field order by selecting a field's column and dragging it to a new position. For example, if we want to look up an employee's phone number, it might be useful to see the Phone# field next to the employee names. Follow these steps to move the Phone# field:

1. Click the Phone# field name to select the entire column.

2. Point to the Phone# field name, hold down the left mouse button, and drag the field to the left. As you move the field, Access highlights the divider lines between columns to indicate the new position of the Phone# field.

3. When the divider line to the right of the Last Name field is highlighted, release the mouse button. As you can see here, the Phone# field moves to its new position:

Hiding and unhiding fields

Sometimes you might want to simplify the display by hiding one or more fields. Simply select the field's column and choose Hide Columns from the Format menu. To redisplay the field, choose Show Columns from the Format menu.

4. For more practice, move the Phone# field back to its original position between the Zip and First Day fields.

Moving fields in datasheet view does not affect the data or change the basic structure of the table.

Sorting Records

The Employees table is short enough that we can view all of its records on the screen at one time. But we may need to work with tables, such as mailing lists, that contain several hundred or even several thousand records. In those tables, one way to easily locate a specific record or set of records is to sort the table on a particular field. Try this:

1. Click the Last Name field name to select that column.

The Sort Ascending and Sort Descending buttons

2. Click the Sort Ascending button on the toolbar to sort starting with A or the lowest digit, or click the Sort Descending button to sort starting with Z or the highest digit.

Sorting on more than one column

To sort the records on more than one column, we must first arrange the columns so that they appear in the table in the order of the sort. For example, to sort a table of invoice data in descending order of sales amount within a region, first move the fields so that they appear side-by-side with the region column to the left of the sales amount column (see the facing page). Then select the two columns and click the Sort Descending button. Access sorts the records first into descending order by region and then into descending order by sales amount within each region.

Ending an Access Session

Well, that's a lot of work for one chapter, and you're probably ready for a break. When we finish working with Access, all we have to do is quit. We don't need to worry about saving the information in open database tables; Access updates the table files one record at a time as we enter or edit records. Let's quit Access now:

1. Quit Access by double-clicking the program's Control menu icon. (You can also choose Exit from the File menu.)

2. If Access asks whether you want to save any layout changes you have made, click Yes.

More About Access

Create forms to facilitate data entry and minimize risk of error

Use queries to select records and fields

Group records in reports in various ways

Calculate totals and other summary statistics

Use a report wizard to create mailing labels

Customers

Cust#: 028   Name: Western Construction Co.
Phone#: 334-7965

Address: 2611 Central Way
City: Lakewood   Zip: 98403

Phonelist   4/30/95

Last Name	First Name	Phone#
Talbot	Carol	334-7625
Westerman	Ron	335-1326
Anderson	Fred	832-8779
Bright	Lance	334-6683
Talbot	Richard	334-7625
Gardner	Linda	334-6754
Davis	Jeffrey	334-9297
Bray	Jonathan	334-0180

Jobs Grouped By Customer

30-Apr-95

Cust#	Job#	Name	Location	Status	Date Completed	Amount of Invoice
028						
	018146A	Western Const. #22	Derby Downs lot #8	Complete		$5,260.76
	018313A	Western Const. #25	Derby Downs lot #9	Complete		$5,295.14
	019449A	Western Const. #30	High Ridge #29	50% Shingled		$0.00
						$10,555.90
						47.03%

Fred Anderson
943 Spruce Circle
Lakewood, WA 98403

Jonathan Bray
5941 Hilltop Road
Lakewood, WA 98403

Lance Bright
148 Center St, #B211
Pinedale, WA 98415

$2,888.26
$0.00
$0.00
$2,888.26
12.87%

Jeffrey Davis
1171 Simpson Heights
Lakewood, WA 98403

Linda Gardner
8841 Market Street
Lakewood, WA 98403

Richard Talbot
1109 Emerson Way
Lakewood, WA 98403

$9,002.88
$0.00
$9,002.88
40.11%

Carol Talbot
1109 Emerson Way
Lakewood, WA 98403

Ron Westerman
1419 Ivy Drive
Pinedale, WA 98415

1

Simple tables like the one we created in Chapter 8 will probably meet many of your needs. However, relational databases like Access enable us to manipulate tables so that we can easily access the information they contain. In this chapter, we look at more ways to work with Access.

Creating One Table Based on Another

Databases often consist of several tables with the same general characteristics. For example, the database for the roofing company might include one table with information about employees and another with information about customers. We don't want to spend a lot of time recreating the structure of the Employees table for the Customers table, and with Access we don't have to. We can copy the structure of an existing table to create a new one. Here's how to copy the Employees table structure to create the Customers table:

The Open Database button

1. With Access loaded, click the Open Database button on the toolbar. Access displays this dialog box:

Copying records

When you want to copy a record from one table to another, you can use the Copy and Paste buttons, provided fields in the two tables are of compatible types. If Access has a problem when pasting the record, it puts the record in a Paste Errors table. By scrutinizing the Paste Errors table, you can usually discover the problem and fix it. You can then cut and paste the record from the Paste Errors table into the desired table.

2. In the File Name list, double-click ROOFS.MDB to display the Roofs database window, which now lists the Employees table.

3. With Employees selected in the database window, click the Copy button on the toolbar.

4. Click the Paste button on the toolbar to display the Paste Table As dialog box.

5. In the Table Name edit box, type *Customers*, select the Structure Only option, and then click OK. Access adds the Customers table to the list in the database window.

6. Select Customers and click Design to display the new table in design view.

Now we need to make some field adjustments:

1. Change the *EmployeeID* field name to *CustomerID*, change the word *employee* in this field's Description column to *customer*, and change this field's Caption property to *Cust#*.

Editing field names and captions

2. Select the SocialSecurityNumber field by clicking its row selector and press the Delete key to delete it. Then delete the First-Name and DateHired fields.

3. Change *LastName* to *Name*, change the field size of this field to *30*, and change the Caption property to *Name*.

4. Change the *HomePhone* field name to *Phone*. The table structure now looks like this:

```
                           Table: Customers
     Field Name          Data Type              Description
 CustomerID              Number      Unique 3-character number identifies each customer
 Name                    Text
 Address                 Text
 City                    Text
 PostalCode              Text
 Phone                   Text

                          Field Properties
 Field Size        20
 Format
 Input Mask        000\-0000;;
 Caption           Phone#
 Default Value                            A field name can be up to 64
 Validation Rule                          characters long, including spaces.
 Validation Text                          Press F1 for help on field names.
 Required          Yes
 Allow Zero Length No
 Indexed           No
```

5. Click the Datasheet View button on the toolbar and when Access prompts you to save the table, click OK.

Copy with caution

Copying the structure of simple tables is relatively easy, but as you begin to create more complex tables, you'll need to consider carefully such characteristics as primary keys and validation rules, as well as the applicability of other Access table features such as referential integrity, which we discuss on page 204. In the meantime, you can see that this technique is a great way of streamlining the table-creation process.

Creating Forms

In Chapter 8, you got a taste of how you can use a form to enter and view the information in a database table one record at a time. When we introduced forms, we mentioned that we can create different kinds of forms to accomplish different kinds of tasks. We can also design custom forms. A detailed discussion of customization is beyond the scope of this book, but we do want to give you a taste of it here. Let's create a form for entering information in the Customers table. Follow these steps to set up the form:

The New Form button

Form wizards

1. Close the Customers table, and then with Customers selected in the database window, click the New Form button on the toolbar.

2. In the New Form dialog box, click the Form Wizards button to display this dialog box:

3. Accept the default Single-Column option by clicking OK. Access displays the first of a series of Single-Column Form Wizard dialog boxes:

Creating forms from scratch

You can create a blank form by clicking the Form button in the database window, clicking New, and then clicking Blank Form in the New Form dialog box. Access switches to design view and displays a form containing only the Detail section, ready for you to add the controls you want. To add a Form Header and Footer or a Page Header and Footer, simply choose the corresponding command from the Format menu.

4. With CustomerID selected in the Available Fields list, click the >> button to move all the field names to the list on the right. Then click the Next button to display this dialog box:

5. Click Standard and click Next to display the last dialog box:

6. Click the Modify The Form's Design option and then click Finish to display this form window:

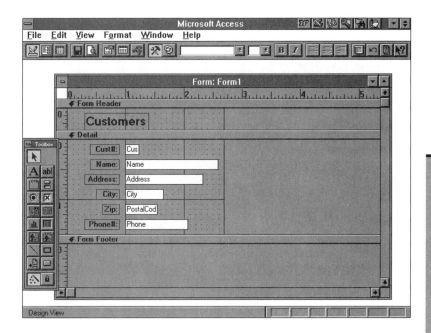

The Toolbox

The Toolbox provides many tools with which you can customize forms. You might want to practice adding elements to forms to explore these tools. If you need help, click the Help button, point to the tool you want to know more about, and click.

We have hidden the database window behind the form window to avoid screen clutter; you might want to do the same.

Saving forms

7. Save the form by clicking the Save button on the toolbar, typing *Customers* as the form's name in the Save As dialog box, and pressing Enter.

The form window

Controls and labels

The form window is divided into three sections: the Form Header section, which currently displays the name of the table on which the form is based; the Detail section, which displays white boxes called *controls* and gray boxes called *labels* for each of the fields you selected for inclusion in the form; and the Form Footer section, which, like the Form Header, can contain information such as a title or date that you want to appear at the bottom of the form. Two other sections, Page Header and Page Footer, are not visible in the form now on your screen. They contain elements you want to appear on every page of a multi-page form. The window also contains horizontal and vertical rulers and gridlines that help you position controls on the form.

Let's customize the Customers form so that its fields are grouped more logically:

1. Click the Name control. Small handles appear around the control's border.

Rearranging controls

2. Point to the selected control and when the pointer changes to a small open hand, drag the control and its label to the right of the CustomerID control, shown as *Cus*. (Use the rulers to help align the controls.)

3. Next select and drag the Phone control and its label under the CustomerID control.

4. Drag the City control down into the space formerly occupied by the Phone control, and drag the PostalCode control down to the right of the City control. Then drag the Address control down so that it sits just above the City control. The fields are now arranged in two groups on the form, like this:

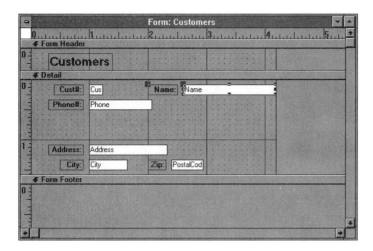

Now let's draw a line to separate the two groups:

1. Click the Line button in the Toolbox and position the cross-hair pointer next to the 3/4-inch mark on the vertical ruler.

The Line button

2. Hold down the left mouse button and drag a horizontal line across the entire width of the window to the 5 1/2-inch mark on the horizontal ruler.

3. Scroll the bottom scroll box back to the left end of its scroll bar and click the Save button to save the changes to the form.

4. Click the Form View button on the toolbar to display the form in form view, as shown here:

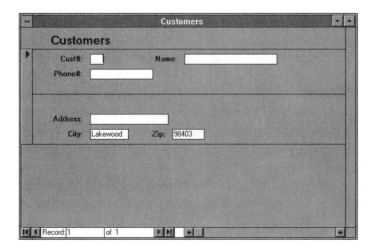

Two types of hands

To move a control and its label on a form so that they maintain their relative positions, select the control and drag the black open hand that appears when you point to the control's border. To move a control independently of its label, select the control and drag the black pointing hand that appears when you point to the large handle in the control's top left corner. Similarly, to move a label independently, select the label and drag the pointing hand.

5. Now enter the customer records, as shown below:

Cust#	Name	Address	City	Zip	Phone#
28	Western Construction Co.	2611 Central Way			8329954
30	Durahomes	4969 Market Street #211	Pinedale	98412	3347965
33	Shurbuilt	966 8th Street			8848742
34	Lakewood City Const. Dept.	28 Central Way			8327865
35	James Bready	511 Shoreline Drive	Pinedale	98412	3348121
41	Marcus Wilson	1701 Airport Way			8323882
45	Roberts Construction	734 Stewart Road			8321044

6. Press Enter and close the Customers table.

Establishing Table Relationships

With Access, we can create relationships between tables so that we can combine the data from more than one table in forms, queries, and reports. Usually the relationships involve tables in which the primary key of one table matches a field called the *foreign key* in another table. You can think of the table with the primary key as the *parent* and the table with the foreign key as the *child*. Usually the values in the foreign key field don't have to be unique, but each one must match a value in the parent's primary key field. Access provides a method called *referential integrity* for ensuring that the field values match.

Foreign keys

Referential integrity

To demonstrate referential integrity, we'll create a new table called Jobs. Follow these steps:

1. Click New in the database window, click the New Table button, and create the following table structure:

Field Name	Data Type	Description
JobID	Text	
CustomerID	Number	
Name	Text	
Location	Text	
Status	Text	
DateCompleted	Date/Time	
AmountInvoice	Currency	

A field name can be up to 64 characters long, including spaces. Press F1 for help on field names.

Field name rules

The field names in any one table must be unique and cannot be longer than 64 characters. You can use any combination of characters except periods, exclamation marks, single back quotation marks, and square brackets.

The Set Primary Key button

2. Click the row selector of the JobID field and then click the Set Primary Key button on the toolbar to make this field the table's primary key (see page 177 if you've forgotten what the primary key is).

3. Assign the fields these properties:

Field	Field Size	Format	Caption	Required
JobID	8		Job#	Yes
CustomerID	Byte	000	Cust#	Yes
Name	25			
Location	25			
Status	25			
DateCompleted		Short Date	Date Completed	
AmountInvoice		Currency	Amount of Invoice	

4. Double-click the Control menu icon to close the window, and save the new table with the name *Jobs* when prompted.

Now let's create a referential integrity relationship between the Customers and Jobs tables:

The Relationships button

1. With the database window active, click the Relationships button on the toolbar to display this dialog box:

2. In the Table/Query list, Access has selected the Customers table. Click the Add button to add a Customers box to the blank window behind the dialog box.

3. Click Jobs, click Add, and then click Close. Access displays the relationships window shown on the next page.

Linking tables

4. In the Customers box, point to the CustomerID field name, hold down the left mouse button, drag the field icon to the CustomerID field name in the Jobs box, and release the mouse button. Access displays this dialog box:

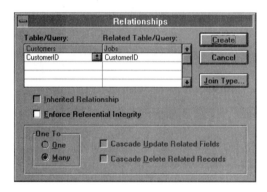

Enforcing referential integrity

5. Click the Enforce Referential Integrity option to tell Access to require that values in the CustomerID field in the Jobs table match values in the same field in the Customers table.

One to many

6. Leave the Many option selected in the One To section to tell Access that for each record in the parent table (Customers), there can be many records with a matching field value in the child table (Jobs). The other One To option, One, means that each record in the parent table can have only one record with a matching value in the child table.

One to one

7. Click the Create button to create the new relationship between the tables. Access draws a line connecting the two fields in the relationships window, like this:

8. Close the relationships window, saving the changes to the database when prompted.

Here's the acid test:

1. Open the Jobs table and enter the data shown here:

Testing referential integrity

Job#	Cust#	Name	Location	Status	Date Cc	Amount of I
018022A	028	Western Const. #21	Derby Downs lot #7	Complete		$6,908.41
018146A	028	Western Const. #22	Derby Downs lot #8	Complete		$5,260.76
0182730	035	Bready Home	11 Shoreline Drive	Complete		$3,392.57
018313A	028	Western Const. #25	Derby Downs lot #9	Complete		$5,295.14
018445A	030	Durahomes - James	924 Atlantic South	Complete		$2,888.26
018967A	033	Shurbuilt - Med One	Corner Stewart & First	Complete		$9,002.88
0193330	041	Wilson Home	1701 Airport Way	Shingled		$0.00
019449A	028	Western Const. #30	High Ridge #29	50% Shingled		$0.00
019526A	030	Durahomes - Mt. View	226 Pine Lane	Felt Down		$0.00
029525A	030	Durahomes - Mt. View	228 Pine Lane	Prepared		$0.00
0301780	034	City Park Lodge	Main Street Park			$0.00
030224A	033	Shurbuilt - Ed's	Lakeview Highway			$0.00
	000					$0.00

Record: 13 of 13

2. Try entering an incorrect customer number. You can type any number in the field, but Access won't let you leave the record until a correct customer number is in place.

3. When you have entered all the data, close the Jobs table.

Often we will make decisions about the data relationships needed in a relational database before we actually create the tables. Database design involves listing the types of data we want to keep in a database, organizing the data in the most

Data modeling

economical way, and then selecting fields such as customer or employee numbers to tie the data in different tables together. This process is called *data modeling*.

Design modification ────────────►

Even the best database designers don't always get the design right the first time. Sometimes we'll have to make changes after we have created the database or even after we have entered the data. This is the case with the Roofs database. As we create the Jobs table, suppose we realize that we need to track the current job assignments of all employees. We can't add an EmployeeID field to the Jobs table because several employees might be assigned to the same job. Instead, we will have to modify the Employees table to include a JobID field. The process involves changing the design of the Employees table, adding another relationship, and entering job numbers in the Employees table. Follow these steps:

1. In the database window, click Employees and then click the Design button to open the table in design view.

2. Select the FirstName field by clicking its row selector, and press the Insert key to add a new blank row above FirstName.

3. Type *JobID* as the new field name, specify Text as the data type, and assign a field size of 8 and a caption of *Job#*.

4. Close the Employees table, saving the changes when prompted.

Now let's add another relationship to the database:

1. Click the Relationships button on the toolbar.

The Add Table button ────────────►

2. When the relationships window appears, click the Add Table button, select Employees, and click the Add button and then the Close button.

3. Next drag the JobID field in the Jobs box to the JobID field in the Employees box, click Enforce Referential Integrity in the Relationships dialog box, and then click Create to add this one-to-many relationship to the database.

4. Close the relationships window, clicking Yes to save your changes.

Now all we have left to do is add the job numbers to the Employees table:

1. Open the Employees table and enter the job numbers shown here, leaving the field for Carol Talbot blank because she works in the office:

2. Close the table.

Using Queries to Extract Information

In Access, we use queries to ask questions about our database tables, to extract complete or partial records from the tables, and even to edit records. Queries that find and extract information from a database are called *select queries*, and queries that perform an action such as updating or deleting records are called *action queries*.

Select queries

Action queries

Selecting Specific Fields

Suppose the roofing company's job supervisor has asked us for a list of the phone numbers of company employees. He is not interested in any other information about the employees; all he wants is names and phone numbers. We can create the list by following these steps:

1. In the Roofs database window, click the Query button and then click New. Then in the New Query dialog box, click New Query. Access opens a select query window and displays the Add Table dialog box.

2. Select Employees, click Add to add the table to the select query window, and then click Close to close the dialog box. The select query window now looks like this:

Query by example (QBE) grid

The Employees box lists the fields in the Employees table. (The * at the top of the list represents the entire table.) Below is a table grid called the *query by example (QBE) grid*, in which you can visually structure the query.

3. In the Employees box, double-click the LastName field name to tell Access to include LastName field values in the answer to your query. Access transfers the LastName field to the first column of the QBE grid's Field row, displaying its name and putting an X in the box in the Show row to indicate that LastName field values should appear in the query datasheet.

4. In the Employees box, double-click FirstName to transfer it to the second column of the grid's Field row. Then scroll the Employees box and double-click the HomePhone field name. (If you double-click the wrong field name, press the Delete key to delete the highlighted entry, and then try again.)

The Run button

5. With the Show boxes of these three fields selected, click the Run button on the toolbar. The result is this datasheet:

6. Print the query datasheet by clicking the Print button on the toolbar and clicking OK in the Print dialog box. You can then give the phone-number list to the job supervisor.

Printing the datasheet

The datasheet and the query that created it are temporary. To be able to run this query periodically without having to recreate it every time, we must save the query. Here's how:

1. Choose Save Query As from the File menu to display the Save As dialog box.

Saving queries

2. In the Query Name edit box, type *Phonelist* as the name of the query and press Enter.

3. Close the select query window.

The database window now lists Phonelist as an existing query. Any time we want to access the datasheet of the names and phone numbers of the roofing company's employees, we can select this query and click Open. Access runs the query and opens a datasheet. If we have made changes to the Employees table, these changes will be reflected in the datasheet.

Selecting Specific Records

What if we want Access to select fields only from specific records? For example, suppose that the shingles for job number 029525A are going to be delivered late and we need the employees assigned to that job to report to the office in the morning instead of the job site. Follow these steps to modify the Phonelist query so that Access will include in the query datasheet only the names and phone numbers of the employees assigned to job 029525A:

1. With Phonelist selected in the database window, click the Design button to display the query in design view.

Adding fields to queries

2. Double-click JobID in the Employees box to add it to the QBE grid, and click the Show box for the JobID field to deselect it.

3. In the Criteria row of the JobID column, type *029525A*. The query now looks like this:

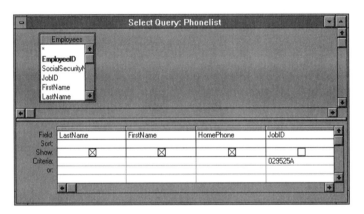

Using wildcards

When you want to select fields based on only part of their entries, you can use the wildcards * and ? before, after, and between characters as placeholders for unknown or varying characters. For example, to find all entries that include *School* or *Schools*, you can use *School? as the criterion. The * wildcard stands for any number and any type of character, and the ? wildcard stands for any one character of any type. When you use wildcards, Access precedes the criterion with the *Like* operator to indicate that you do not want to look for an exact match.

We are telling Access to give us the names and phone numbers from the records that have the value 029525A in the JobID field. (The JobID field value will not appear in the query datasheet because that field's Show box is not selected.)

4. Run the query to create this new Phonelist datasheet:

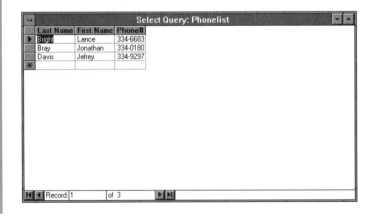

Editing Query Datasheets

If you entered the information for employee number 37 exactly as it is shown on page 192, the datasheet now on your screen indicates a typo in the third record (*Jefrey* should be *Jeffrey*). Correcting the record in the datasheet will automatically correct it in the table. Follow these steps:

1. Click an insertion point to the right of the *f* in *Jefrey*, type *f*, and press Enter to complete the record.

2. Close the select query window without saving the changes to the Phonelist query.

3. In the database window, click the Table button, select Employees, and click Open. Employee number 37 now has a First Name field value of *Jeffrey*.

4. Close the table window.

Using Logical Operators

We can narrow down the data Access pulls from a database table by specifying criteria in more than one field of a select query grid. Sometimes we might want to extract records that meet all the criteria in all the fields (this *And* that), and sometimes we might want to extract records that meet any criterion in any field (this *Or* that). Let's look at an example that uses the And operator.

Suppose we need to know which of the Durahomes jobs is complete so that we can bill the customer; that is, we want to see records that are both for Durahomes and complete. In Access, the And operator is implied whenever we use more than one criterion in a single row of the select query window. Follow these steps to extract the required record:

1. In the database window, highlight the Jobs table, click the New Query button on the toolbar, and click New Query to display the Jobs box in a select query window.

2. Add the JobID, CustomerID, Location, and Status fields to the QBE grid, type *Complete* as a criterion in the Status field, and type *30* as a criterion in the CustomerID field. The select query window looks like the one on the next page.

The New Query button

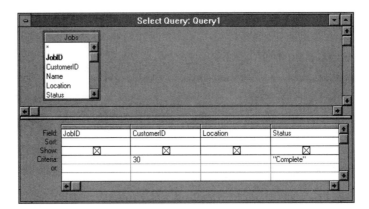

3. Run the query. Access displays the record for the completed Durahomes job:

4. Save the query with the name *Complete Jobs*.

The Or operator

When you want to find records that meet any of two or more criteria, you use the Or operator. Enter the criterion for the first field in the Criteria row and enter all the criteria for the other fields in the Or row. If you want to find records that meet any of two or more criteria in the same field, you enter the criteria under each other in that column of the QBE grid. (Although only one row is designated as the Or row, the Or operator is implied for all the rows below the Or row.)

If the roofing company has many customers, we might want to include the customers' names in the query results, instead of just their numbers. However, the customers' names are not part of the Jobs table; they are stored only in the Customers table. To get the information we want, we must use both tables in a query, like this:

1. With Complete Jobs still open, click the Design View button on the toolbar to display the query in the select query window.

2. Click the Add Table button, double-click Customers, and then click the Close button. The select query window now contains boxes for both tables. Because we have created a relationship between these tables (see page 205), Access indicates the relationship in the select query window by drawing a line between the CustomerID fields in the two boxes.

3. In the Customers box, double-click the Name field to add it to the QBE grid. (You'll have to scroll to see it.)

4. In the QBE grid, deselect the Show box for CustomerID.

Omitting fields from the datasheet

5. Run the query. Access displays the job number, job location, status, and customer name, as shown here:

6. Close the select query window, clicking Yes to save the query.

All the queries we've looked at so far have been select queries, which provide information in datasheets. Unless we save this type of query, the information in the datasheet is temporary; it goes away when we close the select query window. Now let's explore action queries, which we can use to modify the information in our tables and even to create new tables.

Updating Records

From time to time, we may want to change a field value in several records in a table. For example, suppose the Post Office has assigned a new Zip code to Pinewood, and we need to update the Employees table to reflect the change. We could update each record in turn, but an easier way is to use an update query. Follow these steps:

1. Click Table in the database window, select Employees, click the New Query button on the toolbar, and then click New Query.

2. Double-click the PostalCode field to add it to the QBE grid.

3. Click the Update Query button on the toolbar to add an Update To row to the QBE grid.

The Update Query button

4. In the Update To row, type *98415* in the PostalCode field.

5. In the Criteria row, type *98412* in the PostalCode field and then press Enter.

6. Run the query. Access advises you of the number of records to be updated.

7. Click OK to complete the changes.

The Database Window button

8. Click the Database Window button on the toolbar and open the Employees table, where the records for the two employees who live in Pinedale have been updated with the new Zip code.

For a small table, it may be faster to make changes like this one manually. For large tables, using an update query is faster and ensures that all the affected records are changed.

Moving Records

The data we keep in tables is rarely static, and it is often easier to work with current data in one table and archive data in another. The roofing company's Jobs table is a good example. If we keep all the jobs the company has ever worked on in one table, the table will soon become too large to work with on a daily basis. The solution is to have a separate table for the records of jobs that are finished.

To set the stage for the next example, we need to change the Status field values of two records in the Jobs table to *Closed*, indicating not only that the work is complete but that payment has been received. We also need to create a new table to contain the records for closed jobs. Let's get going:

> **More logical operators**
>
> Access allows you to use the following operators as criteria: = (equal to), < (less than), > (greater than), <= (less than or equal to), and >= (greater than or equal to). These operators are often used for such tasks as identifying employees whose salaries fall within a certain range or locating high-volume customers.

1. To keep your desktop neat, close any query and table windows without saving them. Then open the Jobs table.

2. Change the Status values for the records with job numbers 018022A and 0182730 to *Closed*, enter *5/1/95* and *6/1/95* in the Date Complete field of those records, and close the table, saving any changes if asked.

3. With Jobs highlighted in the database window, click the Copy button on the toolbar.

4. Now click the Paste button on the toolbar and in the Paste Table As dialog box, name the table *Closed Jobs*, click Structure Only, and then click OK. Access adds the new table to the list in the database window.

5. Open the Closed Jobs table in design view and delete the Status field by clicking its row selector and pressing Delete.

6. Close the table, saving the changes when prompted.

We are now ready to move the closed records from the Jobs table to the Closed Jobs table. Follow these steps:

1. Select the Jobs table in the database window, click the New Query button on the toolbar, and then click New Query.

Archiving records

2. Add all the fields from the Jobs box to the QBE grid by double-clicking the Jobs title bar, pointing to the selection, dragging the image of the fields to the grid, and releasing the mouse button.

3. Scroll the window and type *Closed* in the Criteria row of the Status field.

4. Now click the Append Query button on the toolbar and when Access displays the Query Properties dialog box, type *Closed Jobs* as the name of the table to which you want to append the results of the query and then click OK.

The Append Query button

5. Run the query and when Access advises you that it will append two rows, click OK to proceed with the query.

6. Close the append query window, saving the query as *Append Closed Jobs* so that you can run it whenever you need to append records from the Jobs table to the Closed Jobs table.

7. Open the Closed Jobs table to verify that it contains the two closed records, as shown here:

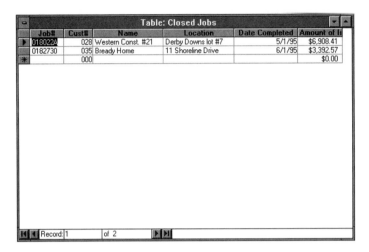

We have copied the closed records to the Closed Jobs table, but the records still exist in the Jobs table. Follow these steps to delete the records:

1. Close the Closed Jobs table, and then open the Jobs table, click the record selector for job number 018022A, press Delete, and click OK to delete the record.

2. Repeat step 1 for job number 0182730 and close the table window.

Using Reports to Print Information

The purpose of a query is to extract information from a database and display it on the screen. The purpose of a report, on the other hand, is to extract information and show it on the printed page. So when you need a neatly formatted hard copy of sorted and grouped information, consider using a report.

To start exploring reports, follow the steps below to create a single-table, single-column report based on the Jobs table:

The AutoReport button

1. In the database window, select Jobs in the table list and then click the AutoReport button on the toolbar. After a few seconds, Access displays this report (we've scrolled the window to show a complete record):

Because reports are usually created to produce printouts, Access displays the report in print preview so that you can see what it will look like on the page.

2. Click the Zoom button on the toolbar to zoom out for a bird's-eye view:

The Zoom button

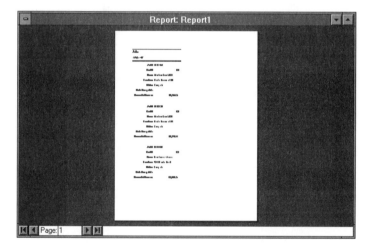

3. Click the Zoom button again to zoom back in and then, using the scroll buttons in the bottom left corner of the screen, scroll from page to page to see how the report will be printed.

As you scroll, notice that the records will be printed in job order. Suppose we want to sort the records by customer instead of by job. Follow these steps:

1. Double-click the report window's Control menu icon to close the window and click No to discard the report.

Creating reports from scratch

You can create a blank report by clicking the Report button in the database window, clicking New, and then clicking Blank Report in the New Report dialog box. Access opens a new report window containing Detail, Page Header, and Page Footer sections. You can then add controls to design the report.

The New Report button

Report wizards

2. With Jobs selected in the database window's table list, click the New Report button on the toolbar.

3. In the New Report dialog box, click Report Wizards. Access asks which wizard you want to use:

The Single-Column Report Wizard

4. Click OK to accept the Single-Column option. Access then displays the first Single-Column Report Wizard dialog box:

Other types of reports

You can use the Summary Report Wizard to generate summary information from a table. For example, you can generate monthly and/or quarterly sales summaries for your customers using a summary report. Simply select the table you want to summarize, click the New Report button on the toolbar, click Report Wizards, and then double-click Summary. Access leads you through the steps necessary to create the summary report. By selecting the Tabular Report Wizard, you can create a report in a simple columnar format that looks like a fancy version of the underlying database table. The data can be sorted on one or more of the table's fields, and a default Sum control displays a total for the first field.

5. Click the >> button to move all the fields to the Field Order box on the right and click Next to display the second dialog box:

6. Double-click the CustomerID field to move it to the Sort Order box, and click Next to display the third dialog box:

Sorting by customer

7. Click Next to accept the default Executive style for the report and display the final Single-Column Report Wizard dialog box:

8. Click the Finish button. The new report looks the same as the previous one except that the jobs are grouped by customer.

Now let's make this report more useful by reorienting the information into a tabular format with field labels in a row across the top and the corresponding field values in columns below. We could make these changes manually, but here's an easier way:

1. Close the report window without saving the report, and with Jobs selected in the database window's table list, click the New Report button on the toolbar.

Grouping by customer

2. Click Report Wizards and in the Report Wizards dialog box, select Groups/Totals and click OK.

The Group/Totals Wizard

3. Move all the available fields to the Field Order box and then click Next.

4. Double-click CustomerID to move it to the Group Records By box, and click Next to display this dialog box:

5. Click Next to select the default grouping. In the next dialog box, select JobID as the field to sort the groups by and click Next.

6. Click Next again to accept Executive as the default style, change the report title to *Jobs Grouped By Customer*, and then click the Finish button. Here's the result:

Grouping by date or time

If you select a date field to group by when designing a Group/Totals report with report wizards, Access gives you the option of grouping the records in your table or query by units of time from one minute up to a year. Grouping by date or time can be useful when totaling sales for a month or quarter, or for almost any other time dependent grouping of information.

7. Double-click the report window's Control menu icon and click Yes to save the report with the name *Jobs By Customer*.

Creating Mailing Labels

As our Access finale, we'll demonstrate another Access report wizard: Mailing Labels. Once you learn how to use the wizard, you'll wish all programs made creating mailing labels this easy.

Suppose the roofing company occasionally sends out information to its employees about benefits. To save time, we want to create a mailing label report that can be used to print a set of current labels whenever they are needed. Follow these steps:

1. In the database window, select Employees in the table list and click the New Report button on the toolbar. Then click Report Wizards and double-click Mailing Label. Access displays this first Mailing Label Wizard dialog box:

The Mailing Label Wizard

The fields are listed for inclusion on the label. In addition, this dialog box displays several buttons that resemble keyboard keys, including a Space (Spacebar) button, a Newline (Enter) button, several punctuation buttons, and a Text button. You use these buttons to specify how the label should be laid out.

2. Double-click the FirstName field to add it to the first line in the Label Appearance box and then click the Space button to insert a space.

3. Double-click the LastName field to add it after the space and then click the Newline button to create a second line.

4. Double-click the Address field and click the Newline button to create a third line.

Customizing reports

Just as you can create custom forms to tailor the input of data, you can create custom reports to tailor its output. Customizing reports is beyond the scope of this book; however, this topic is addressed in *A Quick Course in Access 2 for Windows*, another book in the Quick Course series.

5. Double-click the City field, click the Comma button, and click the Space button. Then click an insertion point in the edit box to the left of the Text button, type *WA*, and click the Text button to add WA to the third line of the label. Finally, click the Space button twice and double-click the PostalCode field to finish the third line.

6. Click Next, move LastName to the Sort Order box, and click Next again to display a dialog box in which Access asks you to specify a label format. You can select the format by Avery number or by the size and number of labels in a row. The list of available formats varies, depending on your printer's capabilities.

7. Select the size you want (we selected Avery 5160) and click Next to display a dialog box where you can format the labels.

8. Change the font size to 10 and the font weight to Bold and click Next. Then click Finish to see the labels in print preview (your screen will reflect the label format you selected):

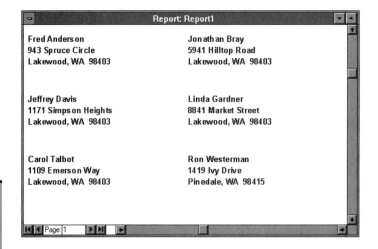

9. Choose Save As from the File menu and save the report with a meaningful name; for example, we saved our report as *5160 Labels*.

Printing Reports

We have looked at reports in print preview to get an idea of how they will look when printed. Using print preview can save a lot of time and paper. If a report is too wide or too long to fit neatly on a page, we can identify the problems in print preview and

Graphing Access data

Graphs are sometimes the most logical way to present data because they allow people to quickly make visual comparisons. In Access, you graph data in a form, not a report. You select the table you want to work with, click the New Form button, click Form Wizards, and double-click Graph to activate the Graph Wizard, which helps you plot your data.

change the report's design or modify the print setup before we commit the report to paper. Here we'll look at modifying the print setup:

1. Click the Print Setup button on the toolbar to open the Print Setup dialog box where you can select many print options, including orientation (landscape or portrait), printer, and margins.

The Print Setup button

2. Click the More button to expand the Print Setup dialog box to include other options related to size, layout, and spacing:

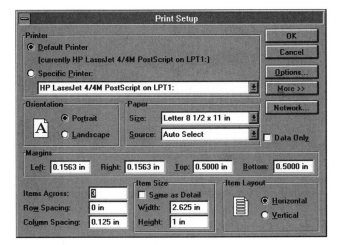

3. All the options have been set to print the mailing labels you created in the previous section, so click Cancel to close the dialog box without changing anything.

Now let's give the printer some work to do:

1. Click the Print button on the toolbar to display the Print dialog box and then click OK.

In Chapters 8 and 9, we have given you only a glimpse of the potential of Access in the expectation that you will learn more about the program as you use it. If you want more practice, you might want to explore *A Quick Course in Access 2 for Windows*, which expands on the information given here to provide a more complete overview of this powerful database program.

Basing labels on queries

As with other reports, you can use queries as the information source for labels. For example, to send information to customers in a specific sales area, you could create a query that extracts information by city or Zip code and then use the query as the basis for the mailing labels.

Using the Office Tools Together

10

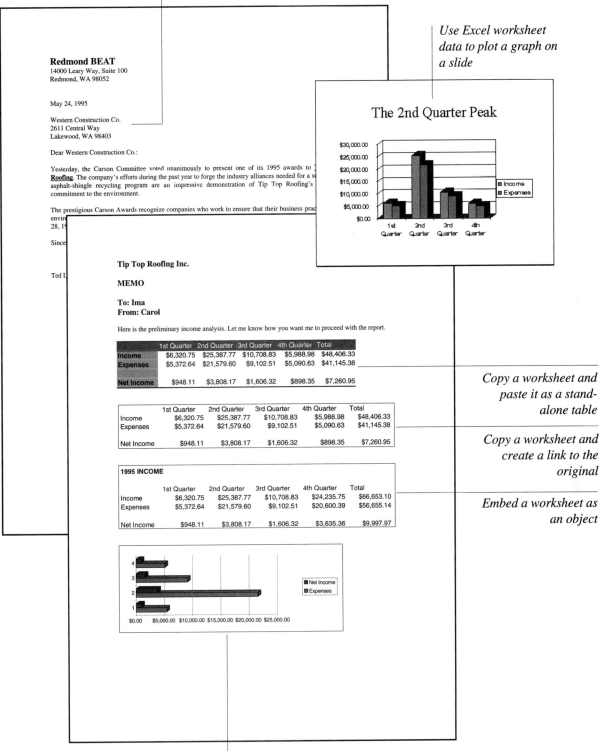

Print form letters using information from a database

Use Excel worksheet data to plot a graph on a slide

Copy a worksheet and paste it as a stand-alone table

Copy a worksheet and create a link to the original

Embed a worksheet as an object

Insert an Excel graph, linking it so that it reflects changes to the Excel data

Way back in Chapter 1, we introduced MOM and mentioned that it functions as the Office control center. Since then, we have pretty much ignored MOM other than as a means of quickly loading the primary Office applications. In this chapter, we take a closer look at MOM. Then we show you how to use its buttons to work efficiently as you recycle information from one application to another. We assume that you have worked through the examples in the previous chapters and that the documents we created in those chapters are stored on your computer.

More About MOM

Provided the Microsoft Office icon is in Program Manager's Startup group (the installation default), when you start Windows, Microsoft Office loads automatically and installs MOM at the top of your screen. As you know, clicking the first four MOM buttons start the four primary Office applications. (The first three buttons serve this function in Office Standard.) Once an application is loaded into memory, clicking its MOM button doesn't start the application again; instead, it makes that application active. Try this:

Activating applications with MOM

1. With all applications closed, click MOM's Microsoft Word button. When Word is loaded, click the Microsoft Excel button, and then click the Microsoft PowerPoint button.

Switching among open applications

2. Click Cancel to close the PowerPoint dialog box, and then click MOM's Microsoft Word button. Word's window comes to the top of the "stack" of open applications.

3. Click the Microsoft Excel button to bring its window to the top and then complete the cycle by clicking the Microsoft Power-Point button.

So much for the application buttons. What do the other two buttons do?

Customizing MOM's Toolbar

Although the Microsoft Office button at the right end of MOM provides access to several features, you are most likely to use it to customize the MOM toolbar. Let's take a look:

1. Click the Microsoft Office button to display this menu:

The Microsoft Office button

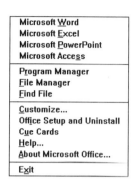

The first set of commands on this menu duplicate the functions of MOM's application buttons. The second set of commands provides direct access to Program Manager and File Manager and to the Find File command, which is also represented by MOM's Find File button (discussed on page 233). We choose the commands in the third set to customize MOM, change the Office installation, and get help. And choosing the lonely command in the fourth section quits Microsoft Office and removes MOM from the screen.

The Microsoft Office menu

2. Choose the Customize command to display this dialog box:

Adding a button to
the MOM toolbar

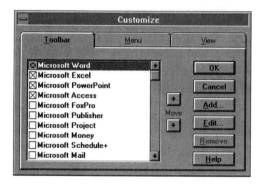

The selected check boxes indicate the programs that currently appear on MOM's toolbar.

3. Scroll the list and click the File Manager check box.

4. With File Manager highlighted, click the Move Up button—the upward-pointing arrow above the word *Move*—until File Manager is at the top of the list, above Microsoft Word. Then click OK. As you can see on the next page, MOM now includes instant access to File Manager.

Moving buttons

File Manager button

Suppose you want to add a MOM button for the Windows Anti Virus program, which is not listed in the Customize dialog box. (If you don't have this program on your computer, substitute a different program in the steps that follow.) Here's what you do:

Adding buttons for unlisted applications

1. Click the Microsoft Office button, choose Customize, and click the Add button to display this dialog box:

2. In the Description edit box, type *Anti Virus* as the description that will appear in ToolTips.

3. Click an insertion point in the Command Line edit box and click the Browse button to display this dialog box:

Help with Office

Microsoft Office has a Help system that works the same way as the application Help systems (see page 25). If you get stuck, you can always choose Help from the Microsoft Office menu to get information about a feature or procedure.

4. Double-click the C:\ folder at the top of the Directories list and then double-click the DOS folder to display a list of files stored in that directory. Scroll until MWAV.EXE is visible, select it, and click OK to close the Browse dialog box.

5. Click the arrow to the right of the Button Image box, select SMILEY.BMP from the list, and click OK.

Selecting a button image

6. Back in the Customize dialog box, click the Move Up arrow to move Anti Virus to the top of the list, and then click OK. Here's the result:

Anti Virus button

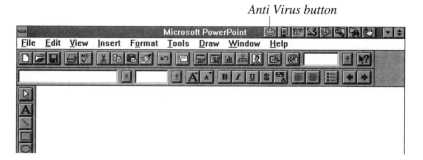

7. Remove the Anti Virus button by choosing Customize from the Microsoft Office menu, selecting Anti Virus, clicking the Remove button, clicking OK to confirm the removal, and then clicking OK to close the dialog box.

Removing a button from the MOM toolbar

In addition to adding and removing buttons, you can customize the MOM toolbar in other ways. Try this:

1. Choose Customize from the Microsoft Office menu and click the View tab to display the options shown here:

Resizing MOM's buttons

Clicking the Regular Buttons or Large Buttons option displays MOM as a floating toolbar that can be positioned anywhere on the screen. The three options at the bottom of the dialog box are self-explanatory.

2. Experiment with the Toolbar Button Size options and then return the MOM toolbar to its usual size and location.

Customizing the Microsoft Office Menu

You can use the Menu tab of the Customize dialog box to tailor the Microsoft Office menu to your needs, though you don't have complete control over this menu the way you do over the toolbar. Follow these steps:

1. Choose Customize from the Microsoft Office menu and click the Menu tab to display these options:

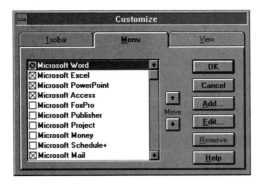

Removing menu items → 2. Scroll the list until you see File Manager and click its check box to deselect it.

Adding menu items → 3. Select Calculator and Print Manager and then scroll the list and deselect Find File.

4. Click OK to close the dialog box and then click the Microsoft Office button to view your changes to the menu:

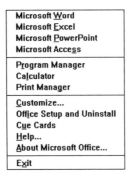

Finding Files

The only MOM button we haven't yet discussed is the Find File button. All the open applications include a Find File command on their File menus, but this button is an easy way of locating the file you need when you are jumping back and forth between applications. In the next example, we'll give you your first taste of how to use the Office tools together. Follow these steps to set up a Word memo in which we will insert an Excel worksheet:

1. Switch to Word and type the following, pressing Enter twice after the last line:

   Tip Top Roofing Inc.

   MEMO

   To: Ima
   From: Carol

   Here is the preliminary income analysis. Let me know how you want me to proceed with the report.

2. Format the first four lines (the memo header) to make them stand out and then save the document with the name *memo1*.

3. Now press Ctrl+End to move to the end of the document and click the Find File button on MOM's toolbar to display the dialog box shown here:

The Find File button

If you see the Find File dialog box instead, someone has already conducted a search on your computer. Click the Search button to display the Search dialog box.

4. You want to find the workbook containing Tip Top Roofing's income analysis, which is stored somewhere in the MSOFFICE\-EXCEL directory. In the Search For section, change the File Name setting to **.xls* and enter *c:\msoffice\excel* as the Location setting. Then select the Rebuild File List and Include Subdirectories options to tell Office to conduct a new search, and click OK. Office searches the specified directory and its subdirectories for any files with an XLS extension and then displays the Find File dialog box, which lists the requested files.

Including subdirectories in a search

Previewing a found file

5. JOBS95.XLS looks like the file you want but just to be sure, check that Preview is selected in the View list and click the filename in the Listed Files box to preview it, like this:

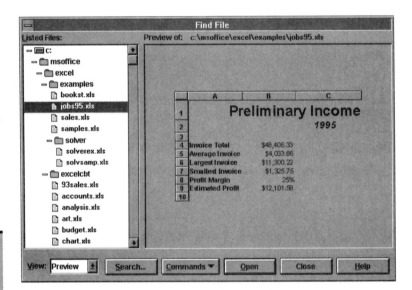

Find File options

In addition to previewing a selected file in the Find File dialog box, you can view its summary information or view information such as its size or date by changing the View setting. Clicking the Commands button displays a menu from which you can print the selected file, copy it, or delete it. You can also access the dialog box displayed when you choose Options from the Tools menu and specify how files are to be sorted in the Find File dialog box.

6. Click the Open button to activate Excel and open JOBS95.XLS.

Now let's copy part of the workbook and paste it in the memo:

1. Click the Annual sheet tab, select A3:F7, and then click the Copy button on the toolbar.

2. Click MOM's Microsoft Word button to switch to Word.

3. With the insertion point at the end of MEMO1.DOC, click the Paste button to insert the copied range in the document as a Word table.

4. As a finishing touch, click anywhere in the table and choose Select Table from the Table menu. Then choose Table AutoFormat from the Table menu and double-click Classic 2. Here are the results:

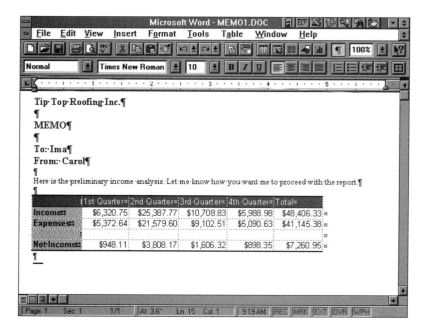

5. Save the document.

Creating Compound Documents

As you have just seen, when we simply paste information from a worksheet into a Word document, the information is translated into a Word table. We could create the information in Word and get the same result, but when the data already exists in Excel, we can save ourselves a lot of typing by recycling the information instead. However, the power of the Office applications far exceeds this simple kind of copy-and-paste recycling. With Office, we can create *compound documents* that are a patchwork of pieces created in the different Office applications.

Compound documents allow us to maintain information in files that can be manipulated by the application that created them but also use that information in files created by other applications. For example, if we want to use an Excel worksheet that relies on an IF function in a Word report, copying and pasting the worksheet would freeze the results of the function. If we later

AutoFormat options

If you apply an autoformat to a table and don't like the result, choose the Table AutoFormat command again and select another format or select (none) from the top of the Formats list. If you like parts of an autoformat and not others, try selecting and deselecting the options in the Formats To Apply section. If an autoformat doesn't quite work with the way data is arranged in your table, try selecting and deselecting the options in the Apply Special Formats To section.

updated the worksheet so that the IF function produced new results, we would have to copy and paste the worksheet again to update the Word report. By creating a compound document, we can ensure that the report always reflects the latest results of the worksheet's IF function.

What Is OLE?

In Office, compound documents are made possible by *Object Linking and Embedding* (OLE). We don't have to be OLE experts to create compound documents, but understanding a bit about the concept of OLE helps us decide which of a couple of different methods to use to create them. So here is a quick run-down.

Objects

An *object* is an item or an element of a document. It can be a block of text, a graphic, a table, a chart, and so on. Associated with each object is presentation data, which determines how the object is displayed, and native data, which determines its content. The application that creates the object is called the *server*. The server donates the object to the *client*, which is sometimes called the *container* because it contains the object.

Linking vs. embedding

To create a compound document, we can *link* an object to the document, or we can *embed* the object. When we link information that is stored in a separate file to a compound document, the compound document contains the information's presentation data and a reference that tells where to find the file containing the information's content. The compound document does not store the content itself. When we embed information, that information is not stored as a separate file. Both its presentation data and its content are stored in the compound document.

When to link

So how does all this influence how we go about creating compound documents? If the object we want to use in compound documents is likely to change and we want to be sure that every instance of the object in every compound document where the information is used reflects the changes, it is best to create the information in its own file and then link the file where it's needed, provided all the compound documents will have access to the file. If the information is not going to change, embedding might be the best way to go because embedded information can be edited in the compound document without the original file

When to embed

having to be present. Bear in mind, however, that compound documents with embedded objects can get very large.

So that's the scoop on OLE. Now let's see how we might go about creating a few compound documents. As you work your way through the following sections, bear in mind that you can quickly run out of computer resources and memory when you are hopping in and out of open applications and working on several documents. We occasionally tell you to close an application we are not going to use for a while. If your computer has lots of memory, you might be able to ignore these instructions. If your machine is short on memory, however, you will probably have to limit the number of applications and documents you have open at one time.

Memory considerations

Recycling Excel Worksheets

You have seen how to add an Excel worksheet to a Word document when you don't need to maintain a link to the worksheet information in Excel. In this section, we'll look at other ways to recycle Excel worksheets. The techniques you'll learn here also apply to the other Office tools, which we'll briefly cover in later sections.

Adding Excel Worksheets to Word Documents

To demonstrate a couple of ways of creating compound documents, we'll use the memo now on your screen and the Annual worksheet in the JOBS95.XLS workbook. Follow these steps to link the worksheet information:

1. Switch to PowerPoint and double-click the Control menu icon to close the application.

2. Back in Word, press Ctrl+End to move to the end of the memo and then press Enter twice.

3. Click MOM's Microsoft Excel button to switch to the open JOBS95.XLS workbook in Excel, be sure A3:F7 is still selected on the Annual worksheet, and click the Copy button.

Linking an Excel worksheet

4. Click MOM's Microsoft Word button to switch back to the memo, and choose Paste Special from the Edit menu to display this dialog box:

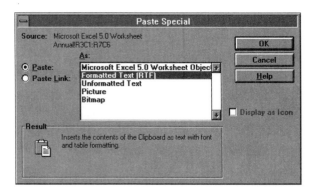

5. Select the Paste Link option, select Microsoft Excel 5.0 Worksheet Object in the As list, and click OK. Word pastes another copy of the worksheet selection into the memo, this time linking the copy to the original worksheet.

We'll test the worksheet link in a moment. For now, let's embed a copy of the same range so that we can explore yet another technique. The following technique will embed the active sheet of the selected workbook, so to avoid embedding the Annual worksheet's graph as well as the income statement, first move the graph to a different sheet and save the workbook with the Annual sheet active:

1. Click the Microsoft Excel button to display JOBS95.XLS and move the graph to another sheet by clicking the graph to select it, clicking the Cut button, clicking the Sheet4 tab, and clicking the Paste button. Double-click the Sheet4 tab and name the sheet *Graph* (see page 107).

2. Move to cell A1 on the Annual sheet and click the Save button to save the workbook with that sheet active. Then close the workbook.

Now for the embedding operation:

1. Switch to Word, and in MEMO1.DOC, press Ctrl+End and then press Enter three times.

More about linking

By default, when you open a document that contains a link to another file, Word automatically updates the linked information. It also updates the information if the source file changes while the linked document is open. The source file does not have to be open for this updating to happen, but it does have to be available to your computer and it does have to be stored exactly where it was when you established the link. If the source file is moved or re-named, the link will be broken. To reestablish the link, choose Links from the File menu, select the link, click the Change Source button, select the source file, and click OK.

2. Choose Object from the Insert menu. When the Object dialog box appears, click the Create From File tab to display these options:

Embedding an Excel worksheet

3. Double-click the appropriate folder icons in the Directories list until the workbooks in the C:\MSOFFICE\EXCEL\EXAMPLES directory are displayed in the File Name list, and then double-click JOBS95.XLS. Word embeds the active Annual sheet of JOBS95.XLS in the memo. (If you hadn't moved the graph to another sheet, it would have been embedded, too.)

4. Save and close the memo.

To see the effects of the different types of objects, let's make a change to the original worksheet:

1. Click the Microsoft Excel button to switch back to Excel, and choose JOBS95.XLS from the bottom of the File menu.

2. Move to the Invoices 1995 sheet and change the amount in cell E26 to $20,000. Then move back to cell A1 of the Annual sheet, which because of the links you created in Chapter 5, has been updated to reflect the changed amount.

3. Save and close the workbook, and quit Excel.

4. Click the Microsoft Word button, choose MEMO1.DOC from the File menu, and scroll the document until you can see the "bottom line" for each worksheet as shown on the next page.

Embedding documents as icons

An option in the Object dialog box allows you to embed an object as an icon. You might use this option, for example, if you want to include supporting information with a report but don't want to clutter up the report itself with information that not everyone would want to read. When you select this option, the object appears in the document as a small graphic, and double-clicking the graphic displays the actual object.

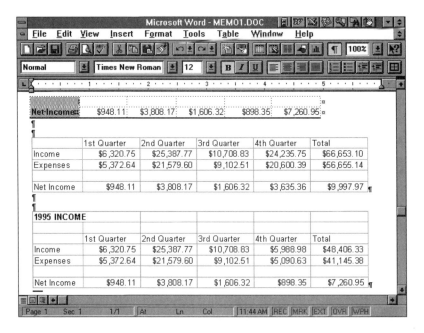

Word has updated the linked table (the second table) to reflect the invoice change, but the other tables have not been updated. To update the first table, we can use regular Word editing techniques, but to update the embedded table, we have to work through Excel, the application that created the object. Try this:

Updating an embedded table

1. Double-click the embedded table. Excel's menus and toolbars replace Word's and the table now appears as a worksheet with a grid of lettered columns and numbered rows, as shown here:

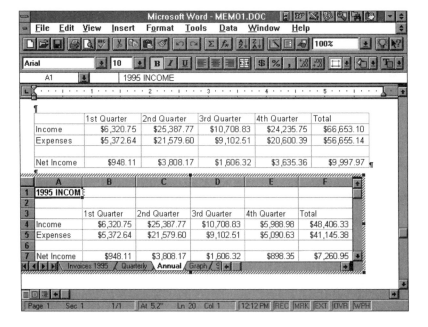

2. Type *24235.75* in cell E4 and click the Enter button on the formula bar. The values in the remaining cells in the 4th Quarter and Total columns are automatically updated because the formulas in those cells remained intact during the embedding procedure.

3. Click outside the worksheet's frame to return to the memo, where the embedded table now looks like this:

Returning to Word

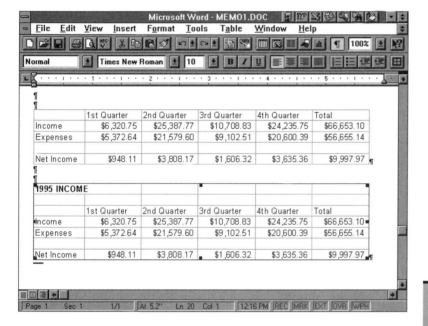

4. Save and close the memo, and then quit Word. (Because of the linked table in MEMO1.DOC, from this point on you are asked whether you want to save your changes, even if you don't make any changes to MEMO1.DOC or JOBS95.XLS.)

After working through these examples, you should have some idea of the advantages and disadvantages of the various ways of using Excel worksheets in Word documents. Let's move on to see how to use worksheets in other applications.

Adding Excel Worksheets to PowerPoint Slides

Suppose we want to use the information in the JOBS95.XLS Annual worksheet in a PowerPoint presentation to Tip Top Roofing's management. Turn the page to see how to embed the worksheet in a slide.

Displaying part of an embedded worksheet

When you embed a worksheet in a document, the entire sheet is initially embedded. If you want to embed the entire sheet but display only part of it, double-click the embedded worksheet to activate Excel, and then hide all the rows or columns you don't want to display by choosing Row and then Hide or Column and then Hide from Excel's Format menu. If you want to embed only part of a sheet, select that part, copy it, switch to Word, choose Paste Special from the Edit menu, select Microsoft Excel 5.0 Worksheet Object from the As list, and click OK.

1. Click MOM's Microsoft PowerPoint button, select the Blank Presentation option in the PowerPoint dialog box, and click OK. PowerPoint displays the AutoLayout dialog box.

2. Select the Object AutoLayout (the fourth one down in the third column) and click OK. PowerPoint opens a new presentation with a blank object slide.

3. Click the title area, type *Annual Income Analysis*, and double-click the object area to display the Insert Object dialog box.

4. Select Microsoft Excel 5.0 Worksheet as the object type and then select the Create From File option to display a dialog box in which you specify the file to be used.

5. Carefully type *c:\msoffice\excel\examples\jobs95.xls* and click OK. PowerPoint then embeds the active Annual worksheet in the slide, as shown here:

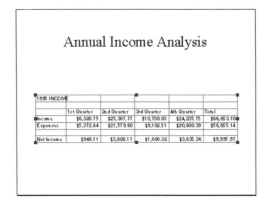

6. Save the presentation in the MSOFFICE\POWERPNT directory with the name *income* and then quit PowerPoint.

As with the embedded worksheet in Word, we can edit the slide worksheet through Excel by double-clicking the worksheet to display the grid and Excel's menus and toolbars.

Importing Excel Worksheets into Access

In the past, many people used spreadsheet applications like Excel to maintain databases of information. Now that easy-to-use database applications like Access are available, it makes sense to switch to Access to take advantage of the many features that facilitate database management and manipulation. If we

---

WordArt

WordArt is a great little program that ships with Office and that helps you produce striking text effects with almost any printer. You can insert a WordArt object in a Word, Excel, or PowerPoint document by choosing Object from the Insert menu and selecting WordArt 2.0 to start the program. Enter a word or phrase, format it, and then have the program arrange your words in an interesting pattern by selecting from a drop-down palette at the left end of the WordArt toolbar. To quit WordArt, click anywhere outside the WordArt text box. The primary application then inserts your design as an object in the active document. You can resize it and move it just like any other object. To edit the object, simply double-click it to open it in the WordArt program.

have current data in a worksheet that could be better maintained in a database, we can import the data to avoid having to recreate the records. To demonstrate, we'll first set up the worksheet:

1. Start Excel, open JOBS95.XLS, and move to the Invoices 1995 worksheet.

2. Select A14:E26, choose Name and Define from the Insert menu, type *Invoices* as the range name, click Add, and then click OK.

3. Save and close the workbook, and then quit Excel.

Next we'll import the data in the Invoices range into a new table called Invoice Log in the Roofs database:

1. Start Access, open ROOFS.MDB, and with the Table list displayed, click the Import button to display the Import dialog box.

2. Double-click Microsoft Excel 5.0 in the Data Source list, and in the Select File dialog box, locate and double-click JOBS95.XLS. Access displays this dialog box:

Defining an import range

The Import button

3. Select the First Row Contains Field Names option and then in the Spreadsheet Range section, select the Named Range option and select Invoices from the drop-down list.

4. Click OK to tell Access to import the data. When a message box appears, reporting the number of records processed, click OK and then click Close to close the Select File dialog box.

5. Select the new JOBS95 table in the database window, choose Rename from the File menu, type *Invoices*, and press Enter.

Adding imported data to an existing table

You can append imported data to the end of an existing table instead of creating a new table by clicking the Append To Existing Table option and selecting a table from the drop-down list.

6. Now open the Invoices table to check the results of the import operation and then quit Access.

Recycling Excel Graphs

The techniques used for recycling Excel graphs are very similar to those used for worksheets. For practice, let's link a graph to both a Word document and a PowerPoint slide.

Adding Excel Graphs to Word Documents

Without any preamble, here are the steps for linking the JOBS95.XLS graph to MEMO1.DOC:

1. Start Excel, open JOBS95.XLS, move to the Graph sheet, and with the graph selected, click the Copy button.

2. Start Word, open MEMO1.DOC, move to the end of the document, and press Enter a couple of times to create some space.

Linking an Excel graph → **3.** Now choose Paste Special from the Edit menu, select Microsoft Excel 5.0 Chart Object, select the Paste Link option, and click OK. Here is the result:

Graphing Word tables

You can use Microsoft Graph to plot graphs of the data in Word tables. First select the data and click the Copy button. Then click the Insert Chart button to open Graph. Clear the datasheet, click the gray "cell" in the top left corner, and paste in the data. When Graph has plotted the data, click outside the graph to close Graph and view the results.

4. Save the memo, switch to Excel, move to the Invoices 1995 tab in JOBS95.XLS, change the entry in E26 back to $1,753.23, and save the worksheet.

5. Switch back to Word, where the linked table and the graph have been updated to reflect the change you made to the worksheet.

6. Save and close the memo, and then quit Word.

Adding Excel Graphs to PowerPoint Slides

If a graph has been created on its own chart sheet, we can add that graph to a slide by activating the Graph program, clicking the Import Chart button, and identifying the graph's file. In Chapter 5, we created an embedded worksheet graph and even though we have moved this graph to its own sheet, Graph cannot import it the way it could if we had created it on a separate chart sheet. All is not lost, however. Here's how to recreate the graph in PowerPoint by using its underlying Excel data:

The Import Chart button

1. With Excel loaded and the JOBS95.XLS file open on your screen, move to the Annual sheet, select A3:E5, and click the Copy button.

2. Start PowerPoint, select the Open An Existing Presentation option in the PowerPoint dialog box, and click OK.

3. Double-click INCOME.PPT in the Open dialog box, click the New Slide button, and double-click the Graph AutoLayout (the third one in the top row).

4. Click the title area of the new slide and type *The 2nd Quarter Peak*. Then double-click the object area to start Microsoft Graph.

5. Click the gray square in the top left corner of the Graph datasheet to select the entire datasheet. (Be careful not to click the Control menu icon at the left end of the datasheet's title bar.) Then choose Clear and All from the Edit menu.

6. Choose Paste Link from the Edit menu and click OK to overwrite the datasheet. Graph displays the ChartWizard dialog box.

7. Select the Category (X) Axis Labels and Series (Y) Axis Labels options and click OK, and then on the toolbar, click the View Datasheet button to toggle it off. Click outside the chart area to see the results shown on the next page.

Formatting embedded Excel graphs

To format an Excel graph that has been embedded on a PowerPoint slide, you must first return to Excel by double-clicking the graph. There, double-click the graph again to open Microsoft Graph, which provides all the tools you need to format the graph.

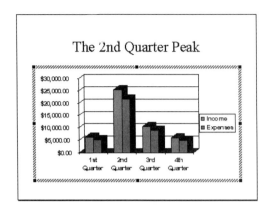

Recycling Word Tables

In Chapter 3, we created a simple Word table to show you how easy it is. As we discuss in this section, Word's powerful table-making feature can be used to build tables in PowerPoint. In addition, we can import the data in our Word tables into both Excel and Access.

Adding Word Tables to PowerPoint Slides

When information needs to be displayed in tabular format but does not need the number-crunching power of Excel, we can embed a Word table in a slide to keep it neat and tidy. Follow these steps:

Creating a table slide

1. Close all applications except PowerPoint and with INCOME.PPT open, add a new slide with the Table AutoLayout.

2. Click the title area of the slide and type *Contract vs. Subcontract*, and then double-click the object area.

3. When the Insert Word Table dialog box appears, change both the Number Of Columns and Number Of Rows settings to 3 and click OK. Word's menus and toolbars replace PowerPoint's so that you can work with the table.

4. Click the second column in the first row, type *# of Jobs*, press Tab, type *Percentage of Income*, and press Tab again. Then enter the following information to complete the table:

Contract	*4*	*$15,941.73*
Subcontract	*8*	*$32,464.14*

Formatting tables

You can use the buttons on Word's Formatting toolbar and the commands on its Format menu to format tables on slides just as you would format a table in a Word document. You can format the text of individual table entries or you can add a border, gridlines, or shading to the table as a whole.

5. Select the entire table, choose Table AutoFormat from the Table menu, and double-click Classic 4.

6. Decrease the size of the frame around the table and make any cosmetic adjustments you want, and then click outside the frame to see these results:

	# of Jobs	Percentage of Income
Contract	4	$15,941.73
Subcontract	8	$32,464.14

Contract vs. Subcontract

7. Save and close the presentation, and then quit PowerPoint.

Converting Word Tables to Excel Worksheets

We've seen how to add Excel worksheets and graphs to Word documents. Now let's see how to import a Word table into an Excel worksheet. Follow these steps:

1. Start Word, open FLYER.DOC, and move to the table at the top of page 2.

2. Select the title, the subtitle, and all the rows of the table by dragging the pointer in the selection bar, and then click the Copy button.

3. Start Excel and with cell A1 of a new worksheet selected, click the Paste button. Excel imports the table as a worksheet, which you can then reformat to look something like the worksheet shown on the next page.

The ClipArt Gallery

With the ClipArt Gallery, you can insert graphics into your Office documents to give them some pizzazz. The technique for inserting graphics varies between applications, so consult the Help menu for more information. However, once you insert a graphic, you can resize it the same way you would a graph (see page 157).

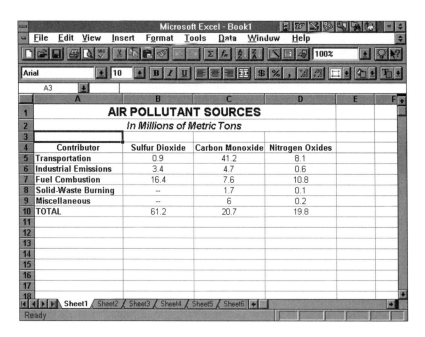

4. Save the worksheet with the name *pollute* and then quit Excel.

As you have seen, Excel can easily convert a Word table into a worksheet that you can manipulate using familiar Excel techniques. If preserving the table's existing Word formatting is critical, instead of using the Paste button, you can use the Paste Special command on the Edit menu to paste the table into Excel as a Word object.

Preserving word formatting

Importing Word Tables into Access

Before we can import a Word table into Access, we have to strip it of all Word's formatting. After we convert the table into a text-only file, Access can handle it just like any other delimited file. (A *delimiter* is a character that indicates where one field ends and another begins.) Follow these steps to set up the pollutants Word table so that it can be imported as an Access table:

Delimiters

1. With the second page of the flyer open on your screen, select only the table and click the Copy button. Then close the flyer.

2. Click the New button on the toolbar to open a new document, click the Paste button to paste in the table, and then switch to normal view by clicking the button at the left end of the horizontal scroll bar. (Page layout view was activated when you opened FLYER.DOC.)

3. To convert the table to plain text, select the table, choose Convert Table To Text from the Table menu, and click OK to accept Tabs as the Separate Text With option. Word converts the table to regular text paragraphs with tab characters where the columns used to be.

Converting a table to text

Using tab separators

4. Choose Save As from the File menu, type *pollute* in the File Name edit box, select Text Only from the Save File As Type drop-down list (notice that Word appends the .TXT extension), and click OK.

5. Close POLLUTE.TXT and when Word asks if you want to save your changes, click Yes and then click Text Only in the Save Format dialog box. Then quit Word.

Now let's move to Access:

1. Start Access, open ROOFS.MDB, and click the Import button.

2. In the Import dialog box, double-click Text (Delimited) as the Data Source option, and in the Select File dialog box, locate POLLUTE.TXT and click Import. Access displays the Import Text Options dialog box.

3. Click Options to enlarge the dialog box like this:

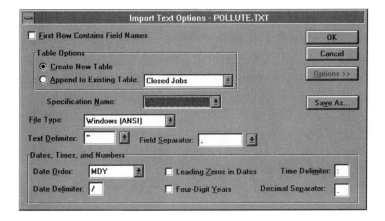

4. Select the First Row Contains Field Names option, and then select {none} from the Text Delimiter drop-down list and {tab} from the Field Separator drop-down list.

Text delimiters

In some text files that are destined to be imported into a database program, fields are enclosed in delimiter characters, such as double quotation marks. The fields in POLLUTE.TXT have no delimiters; they are simply separated by tab characters. Because these characters serve no other purpose, they can be designated as field separators. If, however, the fields were separated by a character such as a comma and commas also occurred as regular punctuation within fields, the fields would need delimiters in order for the database program to know which commas were punctuation and which were field separators.

5. Click OK to close the dialog box, click OK to confirm the import operation, and click Close to close the Select File dialog box. Access adds a POLLUTE table to the Roofs database window.

6. Examine the POLLUTE data in its table window and then quit Access.

Recycling PowerPoint Slide Shows

Once we have invested effort in creating a presentation, we can recycle the presentation text to create an outline that can be used as the basis for a Word document. Here's how:

1. Start PowerPoint and open REDBEAT1.PPT.

The Report It button

2. Click the Report It button on the toolbar. After a few seconds, Word starts and displays the text of the presentation in a document called REDBEAT1.RTF, like this:

```
┌─────────────────────────────────────────────────────────────────┐
│                  Microsoft Word - REDBEAT1.RTF                     │
│  File  Edit  View  Insert  Format  Tools  Table  Window  Help     │
│  [toolbar icons]                                        100%       │
│  Heading 1    Book Antiqua    15    B I U                          │
│                                                                    │
│            Toward·a·Healthy·Environment¶                           │
│                        Ted·Lee¶                                    │
│               About·Redmond·BEAT¶                                  │
│   • Chapter·of·USA·BEAT¶                                           │
│      – Chartered·in·1989¶                                          │
│      – National·office,·Washington·DC·¶                           │
│   • Publishes·On·the·BEAT·newsletter¶                             │
│   • Maintains·resource·center¶                                     │
│   • Supports·local·recycling·efforts¶                             │
│                           ¶                                        │
│                Vision·Statement¶                                   │
│  By·the·year·2000,·all·Redmond·companies·will·have·evaluated·their·business·practices·and·implemented· │
│  any·changes·necessary·to·promote·a·healthy·environment¶          │
│                      Goals¶                                        │
│   • Increase·business·awareness¶                                   │
│   • Encourage·win-win·solutions¶                                  │
│   • Stop·waste¶                                                    │
│  Page 1   Sec 1    1/1    At 1"   Ln 1   Col 1    4:49 PM  REC MRK EXT OVR WPH │
└─────────────────────────────────────────────────────────────────┘
```

Embedding a presentation in a Word document

You can embed a presentation in a Word document just like any other object. For example, you could send a letter to clients about a new product and embed in the letter a presentation that reinforces your sales pitch. Simply choose Object from the Insert menu, click the Create From File tab, select the filename of the presentation and either click OK to insert the first slide of the presentation as a graphic or select the Display As Icon option and click OK to embed the entire presentation as an icon. In the latter case, clients who have PowerPoint can double-click the icon to view the presentation.

3. Choose Save As from the File menu, select Word Document from the Save File As Type drop-down list, switch to the MSOFFICE\WINWORD directory, and click OK to save the document as REDBEAT1.DOC.

You can now reformat the document as appropriate to the task at hand.

Recycling Access Tables

We've seen how to get Excel worksheets and Word tables into Access, but what if we want to get part of a database table out of Access and into another application? This section discusses Access export procedures.

Exporting Access Tables as Excel Worksheets

Earlier we imported invoice information into Access from Excel, but in fact we are much more likely to maintain this kind of log in Access and then export it to Excel for any necessary analysis. Let's export the Invoices table from the Roofs database as a demonstration:

1. Quit both Word and PowerPoint. Then start Access and open ROOFS.MDB.

2. Select Invoices from the Tables list in the database window and click the Analyze It With MS Excel button on the toolbar. Excel then starts and displays INVOICES.XLS, which as you can see here, faithfully reflects the data in the Invoices table (we widened the columns to fit the headings):

The Analyze It With MS Excel button

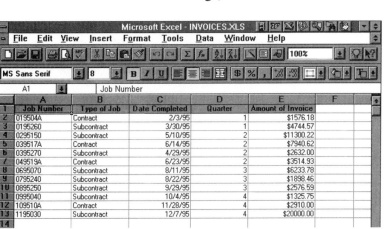

3. Save INVOICES.XLS and quit Excel, leaving Access open.

Exporting Access Tables as Word Documents

We can easily print database tables from Access, but those tables are not formatted in any way. If we want a table to include formatting, we can export it to Word as a delimited text file, convert it into a table, and then apply a few professional touches before printing it. This process is essentially the reverse of the importing process (see page 248). Follow the steps below:

The Export button

1. With the Roofs database window open in Access, click the Export button and then double-click Text (Delimited) as the Data Destination option.

2. In the Select Microsoft Access Object dialog box, double-click Customers and when Access displays the Export To File dialog box, specify that the file is to be saved in the MSOFFICE\-WINWORD directory and click OK.

3. In the Export Text Options dialog box, click the Options button to display options similar to those shown in the Import Text Options dialog box (see page 249). Then select the Store Field Names In First Row option, change the Text Delimiter setting to {none} and the Field Separator setting to {tab}, and click OK.

Now let's open the text file in Word:

1. Quit Access, start Word, and click the Open button.

2. In the Open dialog box, change the List Files Of Type setting to Text Files. In the MSOFFICE\WINWORD directory, select CUSTOMER.TXT (Word has truncated *Customers* to create an eight-character filename), and click OK. Word displays the document, which is a jumble of misaligned words and tabs.

Converting text to a table

3. Choose Select All from the Edit menu and then choose Convert Text To Table from the Table menu to display this dialog box:

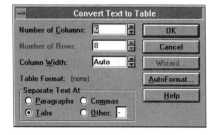

4. Click the AutoFormat button to display the Table AutoFormat dialog box, select Simple 3, and click OK.

5. Click OK to close the Convert Text To Table dialog box accepting its default settings. Press Home to see these results:

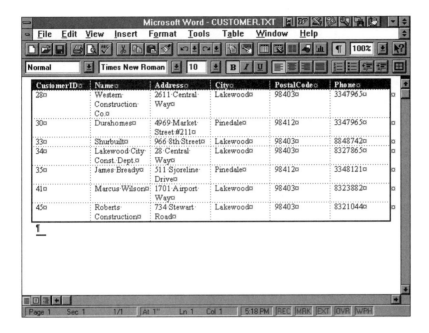

6. Print the table, save it as a Word document with the name CUSTOMER.DOC, and then close it.

Creating Form Letters

In Chapter 9, we briefly covered the process for creating mailing labels from an Access database of names and addresses. In Word, we can use a process called *mail merge* to create form letters for bulk mailings to the names and addresses in an Access database. Mail merge is the printing of a bunch of similar documents by merging the information in one document, called the *main document*, with a database of variable information in a second document, called the *data source*. The main document contains the information that does not change from document to document—the text of a form letter, for example—along with placeholders called *merge fields* for the variable information.

Mail merge

As a demonstration, follow the steps on the next page to set up a form letter and mail merge a copy for each of the customers who have records in the Customers table.

1. In Word, open PRESSREL.DOC, the press release you created in Chapter 3, leave the Redmond BEAT return address at the top of the document, and delete the press release header information, leaving the two main paragraphs intact.

2. Delete *Redmond* and the dash at the beginning of the first paragraph, press Enter twice, type *May 24, 1995*, and press Enter twice more.

3. Click an insertion point at the end of the second paragraph, type a space, and then type the following:

   Please join me in congratulating Tip Top Roofing for this outstanding achievement.

   Sincerely,

   Ted Lee

   The letter now looks like this:

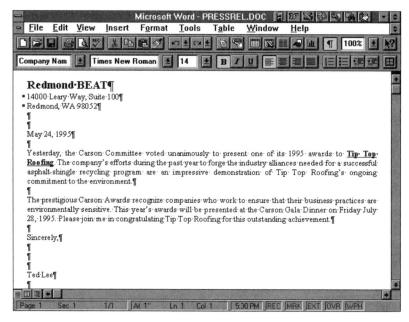

An entire sheet of the same label

Sometimes you may need to print an entire sheet of the same label—for example, for your return address. In Word, choose Envelope and Labels from the Tools menu. Click the Labels tab and type the desired information on the label in the Address box. Click the Full Page Of The Same Label option in the Print section, click Options to select the label style you are using, and click OK. Finally, click Print to send the sheet of labels directly to the printer, or click New Document to insert the label information in a document that you can edit, format, and save just like any other Word document.

4. Save the letter with the name *tiptop*.

Now let's add the information that will turn this simple letter into a form letter:

1. Choose Mail Merge from the Tools menu to display the dialog box shown here:

2. Click the Create button and select Form Letters from the drop-down list. Word displays this dialog box:

3. Click the Active Window button to use TIPTOP.DOC as your main document.

4. Now click the Get Data button and select Open Data Source from the drop-down list.

5. In the Open Data Source dialog box, change the List Files Of Type setting to MS Access Databases, select ROOFS.MDB in the MSOFFICE\ACCESS directory, and click OK.

6. In the Microsoft Access dialog box that appears, select Customers in the Tables list and click OK.

7. When Word asks if you want to add merge fields to your main document, click Edit Main Document to close the Mail Merge Helper dialog box. Word displays the Mail Merge toolbar to help you complete the process.

Creating a new main document/data source

If your main document does not already exist, you can click the New Main Document button. Word then opens a new document and adds an edit button to the Mail Merge Helper dialog box that allows you to go to the main document at any time and type or edit it. If your data source does not already exist, you can select Create Data Source instead of Open Data Source and Word will walk you through the steps of setting up a table of fields (columns) and records (rows) to be used as the source of the variable mail-merge information.

Inserting merge fields

8. Click an insertion point two lines below the date, click the Insert Merge Field button to drop down a list of available fields, and click Name. Word inserts a Name placeholder surrounded by chevrons.

9. Press Enter and insert a merge field for Address; press Enter and insert a merge field for City; type a comma, a space, *WA*, and another space; and then insert a merge field for PostalCode.

10. Press Enter twice, type *Dear* and a space, insert a Name merge field, type a colon, and press Enter twice. Here are the results:

The View Merged Data button

11. Before you go any further, click the View Merged Data button to check that you have entered the merge fields correctly. Word displays the data from the first Customers record, like this:

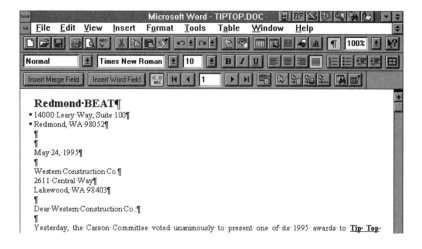

You can cycle through all the records by clicking the Next Record button on the Mail Merge toolbar.

The Next Record button

12. Now for the acid test. Click the Merge To Printer button and then click OK in the Print dialog box to print one copy of the letter for each customer. An example is shown at the beginning of the chapter.

The Merge To Printer button

This very simple example barely scratches the surface of Word's mail merge capabilities. For more sophisticated examples, see *A Quick Course in Word 6 for Windows.*

Sending Files with Mail

For those of you who are working on a network and have Microsoft Mail, we'll finish up this chapter and the book by showing you how you might send a file to a colleague as e-mail. We assume that your system administrator has already set up Mail on your computer and instructed you on the basics of using e-mail. Because we don't know the specifics of your network, our instructions for this section are necessarily very generic. Our intent here is to give you a general idea of the possibilities.

With Mail, electronically addressed messages are sent to and from your computer through your system's post office. Simple messages can be composed in Mail and sent on their way. Or you can create a file in one of the Office applications and choose Send from the File menu to access Mail, attach addressing information, and shoot the file off across the network. Here, we'll look at how we might send the memo we created earlier for review by a colleague. Assuming you have started Mail and logged in, here are the basic steps:

1. With Word loaded, close any open documents and then open MEMO1.DOC, the memo containing the Excel income summary statement and the graph.

2. Choose Send from the File menu to display a blank form in which you can enter the addressing information.

3. Click an insertion point in the To edit box, and either type the name of the person you want to send the memo to or click the Address button and select the name from your address book.

Addressing a message

4. In the Subject edit box, type *Income Summary memo.*

Including a note

5. In the message area, type *Could you please take a quick look at these numbers and get back to me asap? Thanks.* and press Enter.

6. Click the Send button.

That's it! Word and Mail take care of all the details, and all you have to do is wait for a reply.

The Send command is the simple way of sending a file to just one person, but what if you want to send something to your entire department? That's when the Add Routing Slip command comes in handy. Try this:

Sending mail to multiple addresses

1. With the memo still open on your screen, choose Add Routing Slip from the File menu to display the Routing Slip dialog box.

2. Click an insertion point in the To box, and either type the names of the people you want to receive the memo or click the Address button and select them from your address book.

3. In the Message Text edit box, type the same message as before (step 5 above).

4. Select the appropriate Route To Recipients option and then click the Route button to send the document immediately.

We'll leave you to experiment with ways to use Mail to distribute your Office files on your own. If you get stuck, just click the Help button in any dialog box to get the information you need.

Index